JACK

# Shuler's Short Sermons

*Thirty-eight selected sermons by JACK SHULER*

Zondervan Publishing House
GRAND RAPIDS, MICHIGAN

Dedicated to
my folks at El Monte.
the best
Dad and Mom
any fellow
ever had

## FOREWORD

Evangelist Jack Shuler is the worthy preacher-son of a gallant preacher-father — Dr. Robert ("Bob") Shuler of Los Angeles. It was from the lips of his father that I learned about Jack's conversion and call to the ministry, which meant the renunciation of a coveted career in dramatics and the movies.

Later, when he had already won a place of distinction in the broad field of evangelism, Jack Shuler led us in a series of meetings in First Covenant Church, Minneapolis. Tremendous crowds waited upon his ministry. Lives were changed by the power of the Gospel that he so passionately presented. It was evident that here, though still in the process of seasoning, was a young man of superior gifts upon whom there rested unmistakably the touch of the Nail-Scarred Hands.

These sermon "briefs" are sparklingly readable. They are swift, crisp and pointed. They glow with the ardor of Jack's heart. Better still, they throb with the passion of Christ's heart.

The wide range of topics covered, the Biblical insights reflected, the eloquent passages fashioned, and, above all, the grace of the Saviour exalted — these combine to make the following pages a pleasure to introduce and to commend.

*Minneapolis, Minnesota* PAUL S. REES

## CONTENTS

# 1. THE PRISONER

*Let the sighing of the prisoner come before thee; according to the greatness of thy power preserve thou those that are appointed to die* (Ps. 79:11).

I HAVE NEVER ENDURED the cramped confines of a dingy jail vault or suffered the horrors of imprisonment within guarded gates and towers.

My wrists have never felt the bite of steel or the sharp gnawing of tormenting chains. My ankles do not know the feel of wrought iron.

From my birth until now I have walked in the out-of-doors. I have always known what it is to climb the hills and tramp the tangled forests. I have ever been at liberty to bask in the surf, lounge in the meadows, hike the snow-capped mountains, caper through the woodlands, or travel the dusty length of a country road.

If you had wanted me, I might have been found milling with the throng of Christmas shoppers in Chicago; or hidden among the thousands at the Pasadena Rose Bowl on New Year's Day; or walking hurriedly along a New York street to join the Fourth of July celebrators at Times Square.

You might even have found me in Paris, Johannesburg, or Shanghai.

For the confines I have known are the boundaries of this globe. My floor has been the rich brown earth and the ceiling over my head the arching sky. The frail fences of my local habitation have long since succumbed to the automobile, the locomotive, the steamship and the airplane.

If we had chanced to meet, you would have observed my state and called me a free man. We might have exchanged greetings, clasped hands, smiled, perhaps joked. Yet all the while I was a man of despair. I was in the very bonds of misery.

For I was a prisoner!

There are no walls of earth which close one in so surely as those which compose the Bastille of Sin. Nor does the world afford chains which bind more securely than the thongs of evil habit.

And "there is none righteous . . . for all have sinned, and come short of the glory of God."

My dungeon cell was my sinful self, and though I traveled far, my prison was continually there, and I a constant captive. I was conceived in sin and shapen in iniquity; my transgressions were ever before me, as in thought, word and deed I pulled the cords of my captivity tighter. Conscience and Memory stood as overpowering guards to remind me of my guilt and of impending judgment and doom. The brilliant sun which flooded the earth could not dispel the darkness within my heart. The glory of life all around me seemed only to accentuate the hideous mark of death upon my soul.

Then it was that I received my pardon. It came as a sunrise comes upon the darkened earth. It was like the end of a hard winter. It was even as cool torrential rains descending upon the thirsty plains. My fetters fell off. The cords were loosed. The gate opened wide in sweet release.

One who was in the form of God had made Himself of no reputation, taken upon Himself the form of flesh and become obedient unto the death of the Cross. He provided reprieve at awful sacrifice. More than the price paid by the brave men who liberated their comrades at Buchanwald was paid by this Captain of Salvation. Standing at the bar of God's infinite justice in garments dyed red in the sweat of His holy agony, He inquired the payment—and provided it. And the price He paid was His life!

Jesus was bound, condemned, scourged and crucified. But the unfolding years have recorded the strange glory of His passion, and heaven has acclaimed His binding our loosing; His condemnation our justification; His bruising our healing; His death our life.

Who is this One whose bleeding brow is bathed by the weeping moon over Calvary? Of Him the sacred record testifies, "The Spirit of the Lord God is upon me; because he hath anointed me to preach good tidings unto the meek; he hath sent me to bind up the brokenhearted, to proclaim liberty to the captives, and the opening of the prison to them that are bound."

Yes, I was a prisoner, but I discovered God's Emancipation Proclamation. And "he brought me up also out of an horrible pit, out of the miry clay, and set my feet upon a rock, and established my goings. And he hath put a new song in my mouth, even praise unto our God!" Indeed, I find myself an heir of God, and a joint-heir with Christ.

"If the Son shall make you free, ye shall be free indeed."

# 2. TEARS

*And it came to pass . . . that I sat down and wept*
(Neh. 1:4).

NEHEMIAH'S ARE NOT TEARS of mourning shed in the presence of candles and shrouds. His is not the wail of the bereaved gazing upon the corpse-littered streets of a gutted city. His is not the lament of the felon being dragged to the scaffold for execution. Nor does he sob the superficial sob of the tragedian absorbed in the fantastic plot of some ancient form of drama. The text prefaces the account of one of the mightiest revivals of all time. The forerunner of all worthy evangelists beholds the awful apostasy of his people and tells us how a revival started. He declares simply, "I sat down and wept."

Israel, that nation so singularly favored of God, had once written her history upon the golden pages of conquest. Her feet had paced the basin of the Red Sea. Her armies had environed the walls of fortified cities and watched them crumble to dust at her advance. Hers had been the song, "Thy right hand, O Lord, is become glorious in power: thy right hand, O Lord, hath dashed in pieces the enemy!" Hers were the Tabernacle, the Holy Place, the covenant, the oracles, and promises more numerous and bright than the desert stars.

But those corpulent days had felt the biting locust, the tight fingers of famine! The dry rot of apostasy had set in, and Israel had withered. The mighty nation had sinned, and now she shivered within her tumbled walls and charred gates as she counted the wages. The tragic account recited by faithful Hanani settled like coals of fire within the heart of the king's cupbearer and bored like a gnawing worm into his soul. And here is where the story begins. It is the story of prayer that ends in power; of fasting that ends in feasting; of grief that ends in glory! It is the story of a gracious revival. It is the story of a revival that begins where any and every revival must begin or never begin—in tears.

Because a righteous heart overflowed in supplication, all heaven gathered to attention. Because trembling fingers dripped with holy concern, mercy and grace descended. Because the pure desire of an obedient mind gave vent to the sparkling waters of sacred concern, God was pleased to send the power and the wisdom to meet every problem involved. Because a human soul, pressed by the fingers of God, glistened with the dews of faith, God sent a revival. So must it ever be—or never be!

David's reign has been called the Golden Age of Israel. Those were the days when the very heathen were given to the people for their inheritance. Out of those triumphant years comes a prescription. One ingredient seemed so necessary a part of the mixture that David stresses it repeatedly in his Psalms: "My tears have been my meat day and night."—"I water my couch with my tears."

Paul's ministry marked a high point in Christian missionary endeavor. The dim-sighted, ill-formed arch-advocate of Christ had discovered the same secret. "I worked among you with weeping." "I ceased not to warn every one night and day with tears." In a day when every pagan force was at its zenith, the tears of Paul melted the opposition and paved a blazing highway around the world.

From every quarter today comes the query, "Where are our converts?" Perhaps another question provides the answer: "Where are our tears?" Dry-eyed Christianity simply lacks the appeal presented by the "faith of our fathers" that dampened the altar and made the sawdust trail glimmer in the lamplight. A conspicuous lack of tears betrays the fact that our message is all of the head and none of the heart. Until the glowing cheek of the preacher is reflected once more in the glistening faces of the pew there will be no converts; and without converts there can be no revival. "O Jerusalem, Jerusalem!"

Jesus wept, and long years before, one whose heart was strangely attuned to the same Spirit, for the same sinful city, "sat down and wept." Those tears supplement the pen of Nehemiah to tell the beautiful story of God's faithfulness toward those who "sow in tears." They verily prove the promise "He that goeth forth and weepeth, bearing precious seed, shall doubtless come again with rejoicing, bringing his sheaves with him." Somehow there is in human tears a force that knocks at the very gates of heaven and pleads at the throne of God. No pious prayer or sagacious sermon can match the eloquence of tears. Whether burning upon the cheeks of David confessing his sins, or scalding the palms of Peter who has denied the Lord, they bear a message straight from the heart of man to the heart of God. Precious to the Father is that river whose fountainhead is the broken heart of a weeping saint! It is a tide that sweeps before it a band of angels to join the faithful in setting up the gates, rebuilding the walls and establishing that righteousness which exalts the nation. Myriad lips have made request, but there is that in tears which demands of God an answer.

O God, crush these hearts of ours until we weep again. Help us to see what Jesus saw that night on Olivet that distilled upon His face in liquid passion and sent Him down to find eternal glory upon a cross. Mingle our prayers once more with that holy sob that gave us souls in other days. Let our Gospel glitter anew against the background of scintillating sincerity. Then repeat Thy precious promise, "I have heard thy prayer, I have seen thy tears: behold, I will heal thee."

Ashamed of tears? This world of ours
  Might be as well ashamed of flowers;
Skies of their stars when night appears,
  As mortals be ashamed of tears.
For then, if ever, when we weep,
  We waken who have been asleep
And let the flood of feeling roll
  Across the desert of the soul.

We live so much the dull drab days,
  We walk so much life's treadmill ways,
With heart so dumb, with mind so mute,
  We're little better than the brute.
And then some day there comes some grief
  That only tears can give relief;
And then the beauty floods our eyes
  That God has put in rain-washed skies.

Ashamed of tears, when even He
  Knelt weeping in Gethsemane?
We never see God quite so clear
  As through the prism of a tear!
If purity we ever know,
  It is our tears that made us so;
And only they need blush with shame
  To whom emotion never came!

# 3. NOT FOR SALE

*For what shall it profit a man, if he shall gain the whole world, and lose his own soul? Or what shall a man give in exchange for his soul?*

(Mark 8:36-37)

EVERY COMMODITY OF EARTH has its worth. One article of merchandise exceeds another in value; the relative cost of real estate may vary; the rate of stock may differ on the exchange. Yet all these properties are bought and sold on the market, and to each is affixed a price.

Much of the territory now included in the United States once bore a price tag. The Louisiana Purchase found its way into our history books. California, Nevada, and Utah were purchased from Spain. It is assumed that we bought much of the nation from the Indians. And all this for a price.

Indeed, even war is now being computed in dollars and cents.

We have become accustomed to evaluating almost everything with which we are acquainted on a strictly monetary basis. Whether it be an education, a country estate, or a trip abroad, we make the dollar sign the pivot point, and all else is made to revolve around it.

But who can estimate the worth of a soul? Who can fix its price?

The human soul, of all God's vast creation, alone is priceless!

All earth's fabulous billions are not enough to buy

a soul. Place on the counter the cities with their sky-scrapers, hotels and factories, and the sum would be inadequate. Add the six continents with all their precious minerals and vast resources, and still the amount would be insufficient. The earth with its mountains, plains and seas, its gold, silver and oil, its diamonds and pearls—even the staggering wealth of these could not purchase one immortal soul!

The majestic mountains that proudly overlook the plains might well relate their story of the rise and decline of untold civilizations, and yet the mountains are temporal and must pass away. The grand old seas have embraced in their chilling arms the progeny of unnumbered centuries and covered them all with the same damp, cold blanket, and yet the seas are temporal and must pass away. The ancient stars in their courses saw the dawn of creation, and still soar with lightning speed along their ethereal tracks, scarce diminished, and yet the stars are temporal and must pass away.

But the soul is eternal.

Made in the image of God, the soul is ageless. When the hoary hills and seas have found their sepulcher, and the stars have dwindled like dying candles and been smothered in darkness, the soul will still be young. Endowed with perpetual youth and endless life, it shall abide the endless aeons of the everlasting ages.

Of all creation, the soul is nearest to the heart of God. The venerable hills, the surging seas, the blazing sun, the dazzling Milky Way, our galaxy's thirty billion stars, the hundred million such systems within reach of the astronomer's telescope—none of these can compete with the place given the soul in the esteem of our Lord.

Christ did not come to earth for earth's treasures,

though He who had power to make bread of stones need not have died poor. He did not come to gain worldly power, though the kingdoms of earth were offered Him from the Temple's pinnacle. He who veined the mountains with precious metals and strewed the valleys with fabulous gems, who set the stars in their places and holds the universe in the hollow of His hand, saw something more precious than material treasures. When He bade farewell to the heavenly domain and became flesh and dwelt among us—it was for the soul. It was of this precious article He spoke when He proclaimed, "The Son of Man is come to seek and to save that which was lost."

Jesus scarcely took a moment from His busy day to seek enough money to pay His taxes, but He tarried long beside a water-well with a lost soul of Samaria. He sought an avenue of escape when they came by force to make Him king, but He ran not from their jibes and scoffings when He sat at meat with publicans and sinners. He would not court the favor of kings, but His whole attention was gained by a repulsive thief when He spoke of Paradise to one whom society had spewed out and nailed to a cross.

What did He see? He saw the value of a soul! Do we?

Oh, the untold, unimagined worth of one precious soul! In money it were better that one live a pauper and die penniless than lose his soul. In suffering it were better that one endure constant knifing pain all his years if by so doing his soul might be ransomed. In labors no task is too difficult or duty too severe or confining if in such pursuit one deathless soul might be saved.

Strange, there is no heavenly reward promised those who amass a fortune, or who build an empire, or who capture the plaudits of men.

But the Word of God reads clearly, "He that winneth souls is wise . . . And they that be wise shall shine as the brightness of the firmament; and they that turn many to righteousness as the stars for ever and ever."

# 4. THE WEALTHY

*Now ye are rich* (I Cor. 4:8).

AT FIRST I READ IT WITH great doubtings. A poor man, forced to repair tents for his livelihood, wrote it—wrote it to poor people—directed it to those who begged for bread and shivered for shelter. It seemed a cruel paradox: "Now ye are rich." And so I meditated, and in my meditation soared upon the lightning pinions of memory until at last I saw, and understood, and said, "Amen!"

I stood upon the Palisades that overlook the restive sea. The glorious sun, having completed her majestic circuit, glided down the silver highway of the waves toward the western gates. I watched her pause to loose her golden tresses and spill them upon the tide, as; lifting a radiant face skyward, she smiled at the attending clouds, transforming them into scintillating pillars and arches of a fairy palace. Then casting her cloak of many colors just outside the gate, she entered night's portals and melted out of sight, leaving ajar the door, that her admirers might enjoy the lingering loveliness of her afterglow. And deep from out the heart of me came the whisper, "All this is yours."

I clambered up the rugged mountain summit and gazed into the mysterious ravine where the Oregon screams rudely for right-of-way as it thunders over its supporting rock and through its guiding chasms to find the charming quietness of the grand old woods. On and up I climbed to where the weathered pine erected its pointed tent against the terror of the storm. Then, looking up into its battered boughs, I perceived its needled fingers dripping solid silver over my eyes. For the winged seraph who goes about to light each star was at his route, and the light of heaven's majestic chandelier that swings from the ceiling of an infinite dome spilled through the branches, danced upon the water and chased the gloomy phantoms of the forest into hiding among the caves. And as I gazed the whisper came again, "All this is yours."

Then I entered the fragrant halls of a floral paradise just at rise of sun. There were the flowers; and as the windows of dawning opened on golden hinges I watched them wash their pretty faces in the early dews and bend their delicate heads to catch the morning message of the breeze, nature's faithful embassage to that botanical region. Then, hastening to adorn themselves in stunning vesture, they stood upon the emerald carpet beneath an aerial drapery of overhanging blue, robed in garments woven of sunbeams, fretted with silver and ornamented with glistening pearls, until every inch of air from earth to cloud was heavy with perfume and radiant with reflected charm. The playground of angels; the garden of God! And blinded by the excessive glory, I could only hear the voice say, "All this is yours."

And yet I journeyed, far beyond the confines of this world, until *all sense* of time and place was lost. In my hand I held the Blessed Book, and read, and pondered, until, escaping the terrestrial, I found myself ushered into the celestial. I saw the perfection of heaven declare the imperfection of earth. For the grandeur of the throne of God reflected in the River of Life dulled the beauty of that sun upon the sea; and the Daystar, Christ Jesus, rising up, sent all the constellations falling to the dust in embarrassment; and the garlands about the shoulders of the redeemed, plucked from the fields of Eden, smothered the fragrance and stifled the glory of those flowers of earth. And then I knew that though the guarded beauties of our world have dazzled the eye, eye hath not seen it. And though the majestic symphonies of men have charmed the ear, ear hath not heard it. And though the secrets of knowledge have entranced the mind, mind hath not found it. For what shall it be in that day when the redeemed mount up along the glittering circle of the stars and enter through the gates of pearl and file in grand procession down the streets of gold, heirs to God's mansion and throne and crown? What shall it be when, with perfect eye, we see Him face to face? What shall it be when, with perfect ear, we hear His commendation? What shall it be when, with perfect mind, we shall know as we are known? That will be an experience rich with glory!

"Now ye are rich." The Maker of all things has said, "I go to prepare a place for you." The One who painted the splendor of all earthly beauty and veined the strata with imponderable treasure is not building us a shanty. He who possesses all materials and means combines His perfect artistry to pledge that we who trust Him and with patience wait for Him shall not be poor. For presently our greatest Friend and only Saviour shall come and take us home. And then the golden strand shall come in sight, and the harbor. Then the shout of greeting, the song of triumph, our mansion—and Christ.

Behold our wealth!

# 5. THE FATAL CHOICE

*What shall I do then with Jesus which is called Christ?* (Matt. 27:22)

THE RECORD OF PILATE is one of desire and choice. The text in itself indicates the greatest of miracles. That Pilate, or any man, should have discretion with the Incarnate God is the wonder of all wonders of all ages.

In reviewing the scenes of Christ's trial and crucifixion we are bound to confess that the mystery of it all is too deep to fathom. Here we behold hands of flesh striking the cheek of God. Here we witness lips of clay forming vile spittle to fling upon Him. Here we find mortal fingers clinching a scourge that stripes the broken, bleeding back of the King of kings and Lord of lords. Christ is at the mercy of men!

What brought it about?

Put history in reverse and trace it back to its source and you will discover the significance of the first line of Holy Writ: "In the beginning God . . ." Standing on the rim of eternity, the great Creator gazed down through the valley of space and said, "Let there be light!" And, lo, the morning stars broke forth in chorus, and the lightning shafts of a thousand suns sent flaming brilliance to the darkest recesses of infinite gloom. "Let there be earth!" And, behold, a sphere destined to become the cradle and grave of all human-kind began to revolve along its ethereal circle. "Let there be man!" And a creature stirred from out of the dust, stretched, balanced and walked forth a living soul. And God saw that it was good. But it was not good for long. Hell rose up against heaven to vie for God's creation. Sin, that satanic ambassador from the kingdom of all darkness, invaded earth, knocked at the door of Adam's heart, and man, by transgression, fell. And so it was that mankind lost the image of God, and from his loins came murderers, drunkards, warmongers and doers of every lewd and lawless act in the sight of God.

That's what brought it about—this murderous, milling press in the council hall. A degenerate race in a hell-bound world needed a Saviour, and God's only Son volunteered. By way of a virgin's body He entered the realm of flesh. His locks damp with the dews of Jordan, He forged His way through the wilderness and on to Gethsemane. And now, as he nears His goal, and is but a step from the Cross, the drama of destiny takes place. Man faces God across a judgment bar. The creature is met in the council chamber with his Creator. The significance of the occasion flashes across the mind of Pilate, and he blanches. Frantically he looks about for an avenue of escape. But the question is absolutely inescapable. Hear it, guards and soldiers! Hear it, men and angels! Hear it, earth and heaven! "What shall I do then with Jesus which is called Christ?"

An old legend has it that every man, during his span of earthly years, is given his special five minutes. It is the time when the tide rises and the breakers sweep most surely toward the strand. To take that tide at the crest is to be borne to safety. To hesitate is to lose the only current which can carry the soul to its rightful destination. But the tide rose and fell that day while the judge tarried to wash his hands in a laver of water. Pilate's five minutes were gone when he turned back to the howling mob. And as his gavel sounded on the judgment bar, another gavel was heard to resound throughout creation. It was the gavel in the hand of the Judge of the Universe. For while Christ was on trial before Pilate, Pilate was on trial before God; and while Christ awaited sentence from a man who deemed Caesar's friendship more precious than life eternal, a soul was weighed in the balance of heaven and found wanting.

Foolish Pilate! In a few months his robes adorned another back, and his gavel was lightly fondled by another hand! At last he was laid away in an unmarked tomb, and the lips that said, "I wash my hands of this just man," said not another word, and the hands that felt the tepid water in the bowl were stark and stiff and still.

Pilate did not touch the lash that lacerated the back of Jesus. He did not mingle his spittle with that which ran down the Saviour's face. He did not smite the swollen cheek or wield the hammer that buried painful spikes in the aching palms of the Christ. He simply remained neutral. He did nothing. And eternity shall expose his utter folly and prove to all the races of men that indecision is the worst decision of all.

In five minutes this cowering, wavering disgrace to humanity decided to live and die without Jesus Christ.

His was the fatal choice.

# 6. A PEERLESS TEACHER

*For the grace of God . . . hath appeared . . . teaching us . . .* (Titus 2:11-12).

WE ARE LIVING IN THE Day of Grace, and our Gospel has grace as its overwhelming theme and its most vital attraction. No more the frightening "Thou shalt not" of Sinai. No more the ominous exactment of an eye for an eye and a tooth for a tooth. No more a system of bleeding sacrifices offered by poor spirits held in mortal terror. God has not changed—but the schoolmaster has! We are no longer under law. We are under grace!

Christ's coming did not obviate the moral law of our holy God. Rather, He introduced Grace, the new teacher, to her pupils to instruct them and enable them to fulfill that law. On the Cross our Lord purchased the right of every man to be a recipient of full salvation by simple faith. Every Christian finds himself transformed into a realm where human efforts as a means to redemption are lost sight of in the reality that "Jesus paid it all."

Few people understand the true meaning of the "grace of God that bringeth salvation." Many suppose they must go about to establish their own righteousness through fleshly reforms and physical achievements. They hesitate to accept the righteousness of the Perfect One who bought God's favor for us all on a Cross of shame. Yet such is the Bible dictum. "Not by works of righteousness which we have done, but according to his mercy he saved us."

God has ordained to save sinners regardless of human merit, strictly on a repentance and faith basis. Grace is unmerited favor. It is more. It is favor bestowed where disfavor is merited. We went astray, but He brought us back with the drawing power of His love. "For by grace are ye saved through faith; and that not of yourselves: it is the gift of God: not of works, lest any man should boast." God is going to make boasting an impossibility in heaven. No one there will be able to say he earned salvation because of perfect church attendance, or because of a good moral record, or because of a multitude of worthy deeds. The testimony of all will be, "Thou wast slain, and hast redeemed us to God by thy blood out of every kindred, and tongue, and people, and nation."

Salvation is God's free gift to those who will turn from their sins and receive the finished work of the Lord Jesus Christ on Calvary's Cross. It is "without money and without price." It is one commodity not for sale. Nor could the earth afford it if it could be bought. Were all the wealth of all the nations gathered into one lump sum to purchase heaven, it would be like holding out a nickel and bartering for the Empire State Building. God's system of redemption called for penal satisfaction, and it was afforded by the suffering Messiah. God delights in giving. Do you want the oceans? The mountains? The stars overhead? Learn the meaning of the truth "For all things are yours . . . and ye are Christ's; and Christ is God's."

But let it not be supposed that grace lends a license to sin. Read it well: "The grace of God that bringeth salvation hath appeared to all men, teaching us that, denying ungodliness and worldly lusts, we should live soberly, righteously, and godly, in this present world." The law may tell us the difference between right and wrong, but only grace can afford the motive and power to choose the right and shun the wrong. When the mighty truth that Christ died that we might live really dawns upon one, it will make him a bondslave! There is a force mightier than the whiphand, and that is love-force. There is a power more persuasive than the mailed fist, and that is the power of grace.

The law was a schoolmaster to lead us to Christ. In a limited way I learned the meaning of this lesson during my younger years. My father ruled his growing children with a rod, and we certainly needed it. But we five boys outgrew that stage and graduated from that school into manhood. We might then have ganged up on Dad and exacted a pound of flesh for every stripe he had laid upon us. We had the physical strength to do so. But we found ourselves under a more binding law than ever. The very knowledge that our father had loved us, sheltered us, provided for us, educated us, made us all the more anxious to please him. So it is when God's grace becomes the ruling factor in Christian lives. The teachings of grace lead us into a life of holiness and useful service, and demand that we return to God the sacrifice of our bodies, instruments to do His will.

So grace, the greater teacher, lifts up her voice in

the classroom of Christian experience to remind us that "he died for all, that they which live should not henceforth live unto themselves, but unto him which died for them, and rose again."

# 7. AS THE TWIG IS BENT

*My heart is fixed* (Ps. 108:1).

THESE ARE THE WORDS of a holy man who, in the tender years of youth, while guarding his flocks among the Judean hills, made God his choice. It might be considered the final comment in the autobiography of the Psalmist, David, Israel's king and the representative of God to His chosen people. "My heart is fixed," he cried. It could as well be the swan song of the blasphemous, godless atheist.

Age is a fixing agent, whether it establishes a man in his salvation or confirms him in his sins. There is something in the mixture of the multiplying years of life that tends to bring about a crystallization of character and a rigidity of conduct resulting in a philosophy of life that is utterly set and a destiny of soul which is beyond alteration.

The process goes into operation at an early age. Young life is impressionable, susceptible, sensitive. But it contains a will, and according to the direction of that will go both life and destiny. Two babes, blessed with equal opportunity, may, by a difference of choice, eventually be as far apart as the poles. Bent in a certain direction over a period of time, the will of man settles like cement in the mold, and becomes as unbending as the granite boulder.

One ship goes east, another west,
By the selfsame winds that blow:
'Tis the set of the sail, and not the gale,
That determines the way we go!

And, to add another truth to that of the poet, the sail—which we may call man's will—left undisturbed through the voyage of life shall utterly fail to alter the course of man's soul in the sweeping tides of death, no matter how many or how strong the forces attempting to change it.

Thus does one, like the Hebrew, Daniel, in the supple days of youth, remember his Creator, set his mind on things above, and purpose in his heart that he will not be defiled with the things of a world at enmity with God. The strength of his will for godliness overpowers the most unfriendly opposition and erects of every stumbling block a steppingstone upon which he climbs to higher heights of conviction and is made more secure in his determined stand. Through the darksome prison, and amid the ravenous lions, a grand cohesion of holy ambition takes place until the whole heart beats with no other desire than to do the perfect will of God. As the fleshly frame grows weak and a man's weary eyes look back upon a world that is better for his having passed that way, the eyes of the soul with undimmed vision look ahead to glorious fulfillment. "Thou shalt rest, and stand in thy lot at the end of the days." What better epitaph might be placed over his brow than the motto by which he lived and died—"My heart is fixed"?

Another, too a child of choice, may choose a different course. His responsive spirit looks out upon a goodly world with proffered wealth and position and acclaim.

Unlike his fellow, he overlooks eternal values in a mad rush for the glittering temporary. He takes the lower road and hastens to enjoy the rewards of sin for a season. Ere long he discovers that each gaudy gift is purchased only at a terrific price. A little of character and of conscience goes with each transaction. With every wicked bargain the will is seared and the heart scarred. The years that add themselves to his life but substantiate him in his pernicious ways. His once pliable nature becomes petrified. The Spirit of God, grieved, departs from him, leaving him victim to the lawless principles by which he chose to build. He may now be said to be "past feeling." Without the slightest qualm he orders the slaughter of innocents. At the end of life he stands with bloody hands and scarcely dares to glance over his shoulder at the hideous blot he has made upon a world that is worse for his having been born. Haggard and fearful, he dies in the night, entering into a darker eternity where the worm dieth not and the fire is never quenched. His name might be Herod, or Judas, or Pilate, or Hitler. One fact is sure. The passing generations will better understand the sobering principle that drove him to his doom if above his head we place the same inscription—"My heart is fixed."

So goes man upon the earth, the creature of a will that at first he commands, but which at last commands him. It would seem that in his formative years he is stronger than his choice; but in the years of maturity the choice is master and he is slave. Let him cast the vote of his discretion early against God, and the unfolding years will produce a riptide, sweeping upon its giant crest both soul and body into hell. Let him direct his young will toward God, and all the forces of earth and hell shall be powerless to dissuade him in his ever-increasing velocity toward heaven.

The difference between Pharaoh, who in the hardness of his heart resisted God to the bitter end, and the Apostle Paul, who, at the end of the way, looked toward his martyrdom with the confident exclamation "None of these things move me," is the difference between early choices. One could not be called more settled in his ways than the other as they faced eternity. It was simply a matter of direction.

We are not creatures of chance, but of choice. Heaven or hell may be had for the choosing, but once the die is cast, the marching years move in to seal the vote. If at last we gaze upon the golden shore of Immanuel's land, or if we look with anguish upon the charred shores of the land of the desolate and depraved, we all shall be brought to confess it.

"My heart is fixed!"

# 8. THE MYSTERY OF SUFFERING

*For all his days are sorrows* (Eccles. 2:23)

WHEN SOLOMON wrote the book of Ecclesiastes he assumed the role of a pessimist. Forsaking the gay lilt that made his Song of Songs the most delightful love story written, and discarding the grave demeanor that afforded the world the peerless wisdom of his Proverbs, he assumed the atmosphere of darkest gloom to bring forth the most cheerless of all the books of the Bible. From beginning to end he moved through shadows. If there were clouds overhead, they were all of storm variety, and not one owned a silver lining. From his high tower above the Temple courtyard he watched the people at their routine tasks. He marked their endless labor. He observed their griefs, their tears. Joy and laughter were forgotten in the reality of human suffering. The scribe turned to add a line to his account of the life of man. It was a hopeless pronouncement, perhaps unduly severe: "For all his days are sorrows."

Various suggestions have been offered to explain the bitter spirit of the penman. Some have ventured that Solomon had lost out with God, and so expressed his own emptiness. Others intimate that Israel's king portrayed the part of the barbarian, throwing himself deftly into the role of any man isolated from heaven. Whatever the state of his heart or the reason for this unusual production, the writer was not wrong in his appraisal of man's estate. If man's days are not all misery, grief certainly occupies a goodly portion of his time. The bread of sorrows is a diet common to us all.

Human suffering is a mystery. The fact that the righteous suffer with, and ofttimes more, than the godless only deepens the enigma. It is a mystery as confounding as that of infinite space and boundless eternity. It is a mystery as inexplainable as life, as baffling as death.

The Christian mind, persistent in its efforts to comprehend the works and ways of God, has ever met with disappointment on this question. It has turned to the Scriptures for satisfaction and has found there only the solemn rebuke, "My thoughts are not your thoughts, neither are your ways my ways, saith the Lord. For as the heavens are higher than the earth, so are my ways higher than your ways, and my thoughts than your thoughts." Heaven simply refuses to confide to earth the secret wisdom of God in allowing tragedy to visit His children.

The story of Job deals with this problem of human suffering. It presents the sufferings of an upright man whom Satan, with God's permission, deprived of his children and property and smote with such a loathsome disease that death would have been a welcome intruder into his chamber of pain. Out of the agonies of his travail a query is formed and flung out to heaven. Job would know the reason why such adversity should visit one whose every desire was to know and execute the will of God. But the book of Job does not disclose the answer. The final chapters only reiterate the divine truth that man cannot with finite mind either discover or comprehend the mysteries of Almighty God.

Again we ponder this question in regard to the passion of our Lord Jesus. What utter agony He endured at the hands of sinful men! See the blood upon His brow, the spittle on His cheek, the mark of the lash upon His tortured back. Behold the biting thorns in His temples, the gnawing nails in hands and feet. Heed the bitter cry of despair that sounds over the heads of His executioners, "My God, my God, why hast thou forsaken me?" He asked the same question.

But no answer came. The Captain of Salvation, made perfect through suffering, must endure the way of human flesh, and humanity has never received the full and final answer. It is well to say, "Whom the Lord loveth he chasteneth," but that answer is not complete. The mystery of Christian suffering awaits the perfect revelation of eternity. The questioning lips of the God-man grew still, and the voice of the Father who spoke at Jordan and again upon the Mount of Transfiguration was strangely silent. The question went unanswered.

It seems that God chooses the hour of human extremity to teach us most surely the greatest lesson of all the Scriptures — *we walk by faith.*

God would have us in time of storm, as well as when the seas are calm, trust Him implicitly. He would have us commit our way unto Him and lean not unto our own understanding. He would have us believe that "all things work together for good to them that love God." He would have us so rely on His wisdom and discretion that we can add a staunch "Amen" to Job's tribute, "Though he slay me, yet will I trust in him."

The Spirit-guided pen of Ella Wheeler Wilcox has brought much comfort to sorrowing saints in these helpful lines:

I will not doubt, though all my ships at sea
 Come drifting home with broken masts and sails.
I will believe the hand that never fails,
 From seeming evil worketh good in me.
And though I weep because the sails are tattered,
 Still will I cry, while my best hopes lie shattered
"I trust in Thee!"

I will not doubt, though all my prayers return
 Unanswered from the still white realm above;
I will believe it is an all-wise love
 Which hath refused the things for which I yearn.
And though at times I cannot keep from grieving,
 Still the pure ardor of my fixed believing
Undimmed shall burn!

I will not doubt, though sorrows fall like rain
 And troubles swarm like bees about a hive;
I will believe the heights for which I strive
 Are only gained through anguish and by pain.
And though I groan and tremble 'neath the crosses,
 Yet shall I see, through my severest losses,
The greater gain!

I will not doubt! Well anchored is my faith,
 Like some staunch ship my soul braves every gale,
So strong its courage that it shall not quail
 To breast the mighty unknown sea of death!
O may I cry, when body parts with spirit,
 "I do not doubt!" So list'ning worlds may hear it,
With my last breath.

# 9. AN INTOLERANT GOD

*For all these are things that I hate, saith the Lord*
(Zech. 8:17).

WE WORSHIP A GOD who hates.

Our Jehovah God, whose tender care is shown in the soft warmth of sunlight and the gentle patter of rain, whose loving-kindness is expressed in a thousand mercies which accompany us along the road of life, who loves us more than father or mother can ever love us —hates!

God hates sin.

"For the wrath of God is revealed from heaven against all ungodliness and unrighteousness of men," declares the messenger.

One who leaned upon the Master's breast at a memorable supper gave humanity a tender thought. "God loves the world," he said. But no disciple exceeded John in the staunch declaration that God hates sin in the world. To God, sin is a constant source of embarrassment. Our holy God, in whom is light and no darkness at all, detests, despises, deplores that something which gnaws at the character of mortals to render them ungodly and unrighteous. In this regard the great Creator becomes antagonistic. With all His weight He seeks to stamp it out. His wrath is "revealed from heaven" against it. God's great battle is with sin, and He has never compromised at this point. Sacred history indicates that before a human was fashioned, God bestowed His affection upon angelic hosts. They were

God's created angels, holy, beautiful, pure. But Lucifer, Son of the Morning, commanded a rebellion. God acted. He acted against sin. He cleaned it out of heaven, and with the cleansing, Lucifer and his sinning legions fell from the skies like shooting stars. In this, "God spared not the angels that sinned, but cast them down to hell, and delivered them into chains of darkness, to be reserved unto judgment."

God turned to a new creation. Out of chaos He restored order. He formed a new world, and of its elements He made the first man, Adam. He made him in His own image, flawless, faultless, perfect like Himself. But Adam, by transgression, fell. He made in Eden a rendezvous with sin and invited depravity upon the race to follow. Once again God emerged upon the battlefield against his awful opponent, and when the record was written, it told of a God who "spared not the . . . world . . . bringing in the flood upon the world . . . and turning the cities of Sodom and Gomorrah into ashes."

Then it was that the mighty Jehovah turned to a remnant. As an exhausted, heartbroken shepherd gathers the few of his remaining wolf-torn lambs, He turned to Israel. He commissioned a chosen people, formed with them His covenants, gave them the oracles, the promises. He commanded them by righteous obedience to bless the world. But Israel proved false. She forsook the fountains of living waters for broken cisterns which held no water. She bartered her birthright for worse than pottage. She allied herself with God's antagonist, and in the finale, found herself pitted against God. Today Israel serves no better purpose than to pose a frightful warning: "For if God spared not the natural branches, take heed lest he also spare not thee!"

But the vengeance of God did not reach its zenith in these. The scene of all scenes which depicts the limit to which God will go to put down sin is found at Calvary. Paul, in the Roman letter, heralds the sobering fact that God "spared not his own Son." So absolutely did He loathe this disease in society that He sent His only begotten Son to condemn sin in the flesh. He sent this One who never knew sin to become sin for us, that we might, by faith, attain unto the righteousness of God through His sufferings and death.

What unholy foe, with rebel hands, tore the scepter of infinite majesty from His grasp and put in its place the bloody spikes?

What foul fiend stripped the robes of splendor from His fair form and knotted a garment of shame about His loins?

What ghastly adversary in earth or hell had power to call the Lord of all creation from His throne above the circle of the universe to die upon a cross of ignominy while royal blood seeped red from regal veins into the star-lit dirt of Golgotha?

It was sin!

And sin, if unconquered, will send every father's son, every mother's daughter to hell!

"All these are things that I hate, saith the Lord."

# 10. THERE'S ONLY ONE ANSWER

*What must I do to be saved?* (Acts 16:30)

THE MAN WHO ATTEMPTS to discourse on this issue makes himself a target for censure. His critics are, for the most part, those who have found salvation in Christ but who have lost sight of the divine plan in a maze of human modes and physical techniques by which they arrived at the source of their satisfaction.

The question, quite unnecessarily, has caused a deep rift within the body of Christ. When it is mentioned, some minds think of an altar where the answer came after bitter hours spent in tears and agony. Others remember a quiet inquiry room where sweet peace came in answer to silent prayer. Others recall a decision card, a lifted hand, a purposeful handclasp after a faithful pastor's exhortation. Still others are just as certain that for them the solution lay in early home training or in Sunday-school administration. As a result much intolerance has arisen within the body of true believers. Each of us is too prone to lift a sceptical eyebrow and exclaim, "That's not the way I got it."

We must agree that the Bible allows for certain variables in the approach to personal salvation. It considers the fact that humanity is composed of people who differ in temperament. I, for one, do not deny the need for separate denominations among orthodox Christians. No one denomination could possibly minister to the needs of all men. Some people crave excitement whereas others are innately calm. Some require an outward sign whereas others are content to proceed entirely on faith. In this respect denominations are within the will of God, for they minister to the spiritual needs of the world's variety of people. The current dream of a single federated church is absurd. Our physical make-up, emotionally, mentally, socially, forbids it.

Christ considered such variations in temperament throughout His earthly ministry. He suited the method to the person and employed a different technique in dealing with each individual. We have the record of His healing three blind men. To one He merely spoke, saying, "Thy faith hath saved thee." He ran His fingers over the sightless eyes of the second, thus restoring vision. The third He commanded, "Go, wash in the pool of Siloam." All three received their sight. None was more completely healed than another. The miracle was constant, but the method varied. One might have testified that he was healed through the technique of faith, the other of works, the other of water. All would have agreed that beyond any and all techniques, the source of their wonderful cure was Christ.

We poor mortals have a hard time isolating ourselves completely from superstition. Try as we may to abide precisely by Holy Writ, the flesh emerges to post its claims for tangible evidences. The pity is that we become so involved in looking to the mode by which we reached Christ that we lose sight of Christ Himself, the Author and Finisher of our faith. Thus our divisions broaden. We would do well to return to the simplicity of the Scriptures. "Believe on the Lord Jesus Christ, and thou shalt be saved."

But here lies a vital lesson. That little word "on" is full of spiritual connotation which must be understood if true salvation is to come to any of us. It is the English translation of the Greek word *epi* and bears the meaning of vital transaction and change. It would be better translated "unto." Thus the more lucid rendering would be, "Believe *unto* the Lord Jesus Christ, and thou shalt be saved."

Saving faith is a matter of believing in Christ to the extent that one actually changes his location and goes over to Christ's side to engage in Christian practice.

The jailor in question offers an excellent example of such belief. He who a short time before, in open opposition to the cause of Christ, cast the disciples into the inner prison and made them fast in stocks, later was found washing their stripes, sitting at meat with them, rejoicing in His open stand for the kingdom of our Lord. He simply changed sides.

James tells us that the devil "believes." A cheap, shallow "believism" that allows a man to assent to the doctrines of Christianity but remain antagonistic to God's will in his life cannot be called saving belief! Pilate, Judas, the rich young ruler and others expressed their belief in the worthiness of Christ but would not sever themselves from a world contrary to Him. They would not change sides.

The right kind of belief is seen in Peter, who "forsook all" to follow Christ. It is repeated in Paul, who turned his back on the Sanhedrin and inquired of the risen Lord, "What wilt thou have me to do?" It is a belief that results in a change of character and conduct and appears before men in open support of the faith delivered to the saints.

There are many variables among men, and we are not denied any method or means that helps us bring our human will into captivity to the will of God, be it an altar, an anteroom, a decision card, a lifted hand, or a handshake. But God has made salvation to depend on none of these. The true way is invariable, and within reach of all.

"What must I do to be saved?" There is only one answer, and that's the original one!

"Believe on the Lord Jesus Christ, and thou shalt be saved."

## II. FATAL OVERSIGHT

ON SEPTEMBER 1, 1923, the island of Japan was ravaged by the most devastating earthquake in recorded history. The tragic Canto-earthquake began at 11:58 A.M. and continued for more than three and one-half hours, creating casualty lists that stagger the imagination. 143,000 were killed. More than 100,000 lay maimed, wounded and dying in the streets of Yokohama, alone. Out of the rumbling, hissing, murderous holocaust came a frantic plea for help. Ours is a sympathetic nation; a benevolent and charitable people. The great heart of America was touched. In a matter of hours an entire convoy of mercy ships was on the high seas headed for the stricken island. We equipped those ships with the latest in medical supplies, food and clothing and staffed them with a corp of volunteer workers, doctors and nurses to minister to the needs of the helpless millions. Over ten million dollars in cash was also dispatched to alleviate the distress of the victimized.

As the broken little nation set about to rebuild her empire, in appreciation for such help from abroad, a famous five-word cablegram was received at the White House. It was signed by the Emperor himself. It read simply, "America, we will not forget!"

Less than a generation later the whole world was stunned by another cataclysmic and even more disastrous tragedy. It was December 7, 1941. The first light of dawn was just breaking over the peaceful Hawaiian Islands where at anchor lay the vast American fleet, when the drone of fighter planes was heard in the sky.

Out of the blue, hurtling at lightning speed on wings of death, came the little men from "The Kingdom of the Rising Sun." They were bent on destruction, annihilation, extermination. Relentlessly they pursued their attack. Battleship after battleship turned belly-up and sank. Sailors were strafed as they swam for safety. Shore installations were set ablaze. Oil-soaked victims screamed and perished in a cauldron of liquid fire. Two thousand eight hundred of our boys were sent to watery graves in the most savage attack ever unleashed upon our nation by an aggressor. Just eighteen short years after our mercy ships steamed into Tokyo Bay with American good will, came Pearl Harbor!

Japan had forgotten!

There are times when to forget may be considered a virtue. Paul says it is the wisest course to pursue when the child of God is plagued by the memory of his past sins. "Forgetting those things which are behind . . ." is the admonition. Indeed, to forget is one of the most glorious attributes of our merciful, forgiving God! "I . . . am He that blotteth out thy transgressions . . . and will not remember thy sins!" (Isa. 43:25).

But to forget can become a cardinal sin that robs and ruins both men and nations. The Bible relates the story of Pharaoh and tells the cause of his downfall. His dilemma was his failure to remember! He forgot the rivers that turned to blood; the frogs and lice and flies; the boils and hail and locusts; the slain among the first-born throughout the land. He forgot that no man can successfully resist the precepts and purposes of Almighty God. His epitaph reads frightfully, "And the Lord overthrew the Egyptians in the midst of the sea!"

There is another in sacred history who met a most tragic end because he forgot. Belshazzar, king of Babylon had stood to watch his father driven into the open fields to eat grass as the ox; his body wet with the dews of heaven; his hair long like eagles' feathers and his nails like birds' claws. Yet he forgot that God is known by the judgment that He executeth! On one fateful day he defied the very God who had sent his father into exile and made a feast to a thousand of his lords and desecrated the holy vessels of the Temple in a drunken melee. The Medes and Persians found it not difficult to vanquish that fortified city. Belshazzar was slain and his entire kingdom taken captive. The whole story provides the setting for the famous text, "Thou art weighed in the balances and found wanting!"

Adam forgot and lost Paradise. Samson forgot and was shorn of his strength. Saul forgot and lost a kingdom. David forgot and reaped the dread consequences in his family. Judas forgot and died tragically. Peter forgot and quaffed the bitter tears of remorse. It pays to remember! Nothing but heartbreak, grief and woe can come to those who choose to disregard the mercies and the immutable counsels of God.

One of the greatest dangers facing America today is this blighting propensity to forget! America has forgotten what made her great and strong! She has forgotten that her foundation for Democracy with its basic equalities and liberties stems from an early faith in God's Holy Word. She has forgotten that the faith of her founding fathers in the Gospel of Christ effected woman sufferage and equal rights; built public schools and libraries, hospitals, orphanages and old folks' homes. She has forgotten that her strength in international affairs has always been her allegiance to Almighty God;

that her victory in time of war and prosperity in time of peace has ever been the result of prayer and true faith.

We have forgotten as a people that Sabbath breaking, blasphemy, adultery, drunkenness, graft, gambling are in violation of God's great moral laws! That sixteen major civilizations have already crumbled because of the breaking of those laws! That righteousness exalteth a nation; but sin is a reproach to any people. That because of sin God spared not the holy angels; nor the old world; nor the natural branches, Israel! That the wages of sin was, is, and always will be, death!

Ours is a disastrous neglect! A fatal oversight!

Lord God of hosts be with us yet, lest we forget!

# 12. ALMOST

*Almost thou persuadest me to be a Christian*
(Acts 26.28).

HERE IS A WORD freighted with significance. Its value is borrowed from its setting. Its strength lies in the fact that it represents the greatest contrast possible in any context into which it enters. It is a picture word, often describing an agony of feeling, frequently associating with frustration and failure. It tells the story of near-achievement and total loss.

Society has been crowded with people who "almost" succeeded only to live and die unnoticed and unsung. Like Moses in one respect, they blazed a good trail, climbed high enough to overlook the Promised Land, then, having received no more than a glimpse of the reward, languished upon their Mount Nebo. It is a maxim no less true than severe: almost to succeed is to fail utterly.

In Cincinnati I recently heard the story of the early progress of Kroger, the chain-store magnate. When a young man, he and a fellow named Scovanner met in the back room of a little roadside grocery store and drew straws to determine who should run the store and who should haul the produce. Scovanner made the choice which caused him to enter the trucking business and miss wealth and fame by a straw.

The word "almost" sometimes determines the difference between life and death. A West Coast newspaper carried front-page stories about two airplane tragedies. One told of an army transport that went down in mid-Pacific. The other concerned a commercial plane that crashed less than a mile from the San Francisco airport. One went down in sight of the landing field, the other a thousand miles from land. Yet in one vital respect there was no difference, for all aboard both planes perished.

So reads the account in the twenty-sixth chapter of Acts. Scholars differ in their interpretation of Agrippa's words. Some say his retort to Paul was one of scorn. Others insist that for an instant he halted very close to a decision for Christ. Regardless of interpretation, it is safe to conclude that never a more powerful preacher or convincing sermon was witnessed by this man in kingly garb. Paul, who so recently had caused Felix to tremble beneath the impact of a Spirit-propelled sermon, pressed the claims of God's throne upon another dignitary. His persuasion overpowered the king's intellect, commanded his conscience, arrested the attention of his entire being. But the pride of a haughty heart threw up a last barrier which would not yield to the onslaught of God's battering-ram of conviction.

"Almost thou persuadest me to be a Christian." Peace and pardon were just within reach. The hand of mercy beckoned. Eternal issues weighed for one short moment in the balances, and all the glories of the Gospel of redeeming grace availed themselves to be claimed. Yet, like a distressed ship which in sight of harbor turns back out to sea, Agrippa decided to take his chances with the storm. He who was "almost persuaded" chose for time and eternity to remain without God.

Agrippa is but one of many whose tragic ruin turned upon an "almost." Pharaoh, who contradicted his stand repeatedly before Moses; Herod, who heard John gladly, yet ordered him decapitated; Judas, who sat at meat with Christ and afterward betrayed him; Pilate, who would have let Christ go but for his friendship with Caesar; Felix, who quaked as he shrank from the wooing of the Holy Spirit — these are but a few of those who went far, but not far enough. For these "almost" and "not" had equivalent meanings. They discovered that to be less than fully persuaded was to be as infinitely removed from salvation as though they had never been persuaded at all.

"Almost!" In one respect it is an emtpy word, without profit or advantage. Of what avail is it if it "almost" rains, or if the sun "almost" shines? Can a man overcome hunger by "almost" eating, or thirst by "almost" drinking, or fatigue by "almost" sleeping? A sailor not fully persuaded to escape a sinking vessel only becomes a victim to the devouring sea. Just so, the man who is "almost persuaded" to turn from sin to Christ not only slights God's mercy but chooses God's wrath and the final sentence of damnation.

A near-decision is in reality no decision at all. Lips that once spoke in the judgment chamber a sentence that sounded almost hopeful can now only moan, "Once I was at the very gate of heaven and was about to enter in; but now I am in the lap of hell!"

The little bit more, and how much it is:
The little bit less—and what worlds away!

To be almost saved is to be altogether lost!

# 13. PECULIAR PEOPLE

*Who gave himself for us, that he might redeem us from all iniquity, and purify unto himself a peculiar people, zealous of good works* (Titus 2.14).

PAUL, IN WRITING to Titus, inscribes a statement of fact that has been the recipient of as much abuse as any Scriptural dogma. He plainly declares that Christians are to be a peculiar people. In spite of the many and varied interpretations that have revolved about the teaching, it is as much a part of our Bible as "God so loved the world" and "Whosoever will."

If the Bible is emphatic at any one point it is this: there is to be a manifest difference between believers and unbelievers. We are those who have passed out of darkness into light, and we must walk as children of light. We are to abstain from fleshly lusts and separate ourselves unto a life pleasing to God. We are warned against conforming to the ways of the world and are exhorted to be transformed in thought, word and deed. It is to be the badge of our salvation. Christ has redeemed us from all iniquity and purified unto Himself a peculiar people.

But it is at the point of our peculiarity that some have stumbled. They have supposed that we are to affect a peculiarity in dress and custom which our Lord never intended. There are many ways to be peculiar. An

African Hottentot, with loincloth and tattooed body, walking down the streets of an American city would indeed be a peculiar spectacle, though such a sight might be perfectly proper in the Congo.

Our peculiarity is not to lie particularly in apparel. Christ's dress, though not elaborate or gaudy, was essentially the garb of His day. His disciples did not dress unlike the average citizen of the land. Certainly we are to exercise good taste and modesty in all things, but to call attention to ourselves by wearing garments which violate custom is not the meaning of this verse.

Again, the difference does not lie primarily in our manner of speech. Although our conversation is to be chaste and holy, it need not differ from the basic language of our fellow countrymen any more than the language of the early Christians differed from the common tongue of their day.

Nor is our peculiarity to be one of facial expression or physical mannerism. Our Lord's personal appearance was not startling to those of His generation. It was not then the custom to be clean-shaven. Robes and sandals were in the general wardrobe of every man of that day. He did not defy current fashion, though His seamless garment was one common to the poorer element with which He identified Himself.

Wherein, then, is our peculiarity to be found? The verse provides the answer. It declares that we are different in that we are "zealous of good works."

God's people are to be different in the way they react to adverse world conditions. Joseph was peculiar when he fled the advances of Potiphar's wife. Moses was peculiar when he abandoned the ease and the luxury of an Egyptian court for a desert rendezvous with God. Daniel was peculiar when he forfeited the favor of the king to seek the approval of heaven. Paul and Silas, with bloody backs, were peculiar when they sang hymns at midnight in a Philippian jail. God's people have always been peculiar in the way they have faced and overcome their difficulties.

The book of Exodus gives us a significant record of such a peculiar people. Israel's armies were in no way equal in strength to those of Egypt, nor were her battle chariots and war implements to be compared. Yet, upon facing the same barrier, the Israelites crossed the Red Sea unscathed, whereas the Egyptians cracked up and were drowned. The peculiarity which marked the triumph of the Israelites and the destruction of the Egyptians was essentially one of faith. The Egyptians relied on their weapons and superior physical forces, whereas the Hebrews relied on God.

The biography of Abraham is that of a peculiar man. His attire was not strange. His manner of speech was not different. His personal bearing was not peculiar. But Abraham stands apart from every other man in his generation because of the fact that he believed God in the face of impossible circumstances and triumphed over them through faith.

The eleventh chapter of Hebrews speaks of Abel, Enoch, Noah, Abraham, Gideon, Barak and innumerable others whose one mark of distinction was an unswerving, uncompromising faith. Through that faith they "subdued kingdoms, wrought righteousness, obtained promises, stopped the mouths of lions, quenched the violence of fire, escaped the edge of the sword, out of weakness were made strong, waxed valiant in fight, turned to flight the armies of the aliens."

It is the description of a peculiar people.

# 14. THE WITHERED HAND

*And there was a man there which had a withered hand* (Mark 3:1).

NO MIRACLE that Christ performed was without spiritual significance. Never was He involved in a healing but that a sermon went out to His crowd. I am thinking just now of a Sabbath Day miracle in Jerusalem. The Temple is filled with worshippers. Ritual and ceremony are the order of the day. But suddenly the attention of the people is drawn to the side door. Someone is entering. It is the Preacher! And as we behold Him we are bound to confess that all the fullness of God's glorious grace radiates from His Person. The Preacher for the occasion is the Lord Jesus Christ.

Jesus never allowed Himself to be confined by program, nor does He on this occasion. Violating all customary procedure, He looks past the scribes and elders, the doctors and the lawyers, back into the shadows, where sits a man with a withered hand. Singling him out from all the rest, He directs His attention to him. Jesus has found His Sunday-morning sermon!

There is nothing wrong with a man with a withered hand except that he can't come to grip with things. Perhaps that is where our deficiency lies.

The promises of God are yea and amen, and every one is a reservoir of omnipotent power ready to be poured out in our behalf. But we have lost our hold on the promises. We cannot manipulate them to make them work for us. Our hands won't take hold.

Prayer is the mightiest force in all the universe. It moves the hand that moves the world. But we have become impotent to lay hold upon the horns of the altar and tarry in effectual prayer. Our hands are withered.

The truths of the Word are still verity, and still maintain the secret that makes men free, but verity has escaped us. Somehow we have let truth slip. We face a world that perishes, and a society that is disintegrating, and we look at our hands, and they are drawn and helpless. The Gospel of Christ that is the power of God unto salvation has not been appropriated.

As a consequence we have lost our power to grip the world. Those first Christians had a hold on their generation. They dug their fingers into human hearts and moved them toward Christ. They clenched the reins of nations and steered them heavenward. They had hands — strong hands!

Have you ever thought how important hands are to our well-being and progress? Hands are among the most useful members of the body, and are perhaps the most expressive.

Without hands we cannot clothe and feed ourselves. We are so constructed that garments cannot clothe the back nor food reach the mouth unless hands make this possible. In this fact lies a sermon in this Sabbath Day miracle at Jerusalem. How many Christians are spiritually starved because their hands are too weak to delve into the Bible and transport heaven's manna to the famished lips of the soul? We take a little "milk" from the pastor's spoon on Sunday but lack the strength to feed ourselves the wonderful words of life, the meat that builds spiritual sinew and brawn.

Again, we care for others with our hands. They are our medium for extending aid to our fellow man. I am constantly called upon by people — good people — who lament the fact that they cannot win their closest loved ones to Christ. Let us look at our hands. Why can't we extend them to lift the fallen and apply the Balm of Gilead to wounded souls? They are shriveled. We would "rescue the perishing and care for the dying," but our hands are withered.

But the glory of this account stems from the fact that the man with the withered hand was found in the Temple when Christ came. He did not fail to meet his appointment with God. Like Jacob at Bethel, Elijah at Cherith, the hundred and twenty in the upper chamber, he had sought out the place of blessing, and Christ met him there.

The event unfolds. Christ issues an order. "Stand forth!" There is no cure that does not follow on the heels of confession. "Stand forth in the midst. Show the crowd that hand. Confess and admit your weakness and inadequacy. Declare it. Publish it. Victory will never come to those who hide."

If we as individual Christians and if the Church as the body of Christ would enjoy the fullness of spiritual strength, we must confess our faults and admit our weaknesses. Nothing was ever gained by hiding our dilemma. The promise abides, "Whoso confesseth and forsaketh . . . shall have mercy."

A second command sounds upon the air: "Stretch

forth thine hand!" Christ is awakening and calling forth the man's greatest power. He asks for his faith. He asks him to do the very thing he cannot do. His hand is withered, dried, shriveled. But Faith triumphs in the face of impossible circumstances. Where every human and natural force sighs, "I cannot!" Faith shouts, "I will!"

Volumes might be written around the simple statement of Scripture, "And his hand was restored whole as the other." Paul resumes the story in his Roman letter and declares, "If thou shalt confess with thy mouth the Lord Jesus, and shalt believe in thine heart that God hath raised him from the dead, thou shalt be saved."

# 15. SONGS

*From the uttermost part of the earth have we heard songs* (Isa. 24:16).

SINCE THE DAWN of creation, when the morning stars sang together, God's world has been full of music.

The confusion of tongues at Babel created divisions among the peoples of earth which have steadily broadened, but through it all one fact has remained universal and provided a common denomination among all nations. People the world around still sing. The operas of Europe, the cants of the Orient, the weird chants of Africa, the gay rhythms of Latin America, the lyrical ballads of the Anglo-Saxons — all bind a disintegrating world together in song.

Holy Revelation is full of songs. The Psalms are the compiled sacred hymns of Bible times. Solomon's Song of Songs and Jeremiah's Lamentations combine with the many other songs of Holy Writ to magnify the importance of musical expression.

The body of believers is a vast choir whose lyric praises fill the earth as surely as the rare perfume of field flowers sweetens the meadow breeze. Each child of God is a chorister whose lips cannot cease to raise harmonies to his Redeemer. Under the deft baton of the Great Conductor, the Holy Spirit, all Christendom gives forth in full-throated melody a sweet song of worship unto Him who loved us and gave Himself for us.

Every period of spiritual revival in earth's history has

been accompanied by an outburst of Christian song. Love's best mode of expression is that of lyrical poetry, and when heavenly emotion rises, tongues respond in songs which become no less a part of the record than the very movement of the Spirit Himself. The emancipation anthem of the Luther revival was "A Mighty Fortress Is Our God." John Wesley's preaching was made complete only by his brother Charles' singing. The Welsh Revival saw more songs than sermons, and hymns were heard morning, noon and night throughout the length and breadth of the land. Music is sometimes the only language which can give full vent to the emotions of a heart caught in the grip of God.

Today in some churches the hymns go deeper than the creeds, and are sometimes found to be the key God uses to unlock the door of sinful hearts. The very lilt and meter of the grand old songs of the Church speak a universal language which has persuaded many to turn from death to life.

The Word of God furnishes a study in songs.

Moses' song at the crossing of the Red Sea was one of deliverance (Exod. 15). David's lament over the death of Saul and Jonathan has become a classic (II Sam. 1). A song of victory was sung by Deborah and Barak at the overthrow of the enemy (Judg. 5). Hannah lifted her voice in a song of gratitude at the birth of her son Samuel (I Sam. 2).

With a hymn Christ prepared Himself for the awful ordeal of Gethsemane.

The song of salvation is one which every blood-bought child of God has sung. In the words of David,

"Mercy and truth are met together; righteousness and peace have kissed each other."

One of the most blessed thoughts of Scripture is found in Elihu's mention to suffering Job of "songs in the night." When troubles fall like thundering hail and sorrows overwhelm the soul, Jesus gives us a song. Though we stumble blindly through the dark valley of the shadow of death, we shall not fear, for His song of assurance and of comfort is heard, a melody of sustaining grace for every blood-bought child.

But the grandest song of all the ages has not yet been sung by mortal tongue. On the Isle of Patmos John saw a vision of the ransomed multitude. He heard them in the grand finale. "And they sung a new song, saying, Thou art worthy to take the book, and to open the seals thereof: for thou wast slain, and hast redeemed us to God by thy blood," he wrote. When the long battle is ended and God's saints are gathered home, we shall blend our voices in the song of full and final deliverance. Then every wicked force and blighting influence shall have been annihilated, and the song of the broken yoke of bondage, the song of Moses and the Lamb, shall swell upward to the ethereal sky and resound in triumph among the celestial hills.

Here we sing our songs from a vale of wrath and pain — songs of sorrow and of mourning, or of victory in the face of hardship. We sing through our tears. We lift our voices above the lashing waves of a furious sea of temptations and difficulties through which we are called to go.

But in that great day only the song shall endure. With

eye undimmed and spirit forever free we shall sing our song unhindered. No sin; no tears; no strife: only the song!

Then in a nobler, sweeter song
I'll sing Thy power to save,
When this poor lisping, stammering tongue
Lies silent in the grave.

# 16. CURE FOR DISCOURAGEMENT

*Art thou he that should come, or do we look for another?* (Matt. 11:3)

THESE ARE WORDS borrowed from a gloomy chapter in the life of a great man. John the Baptist was acclaimed by Christ the "greatest born of woman." The sledge-hammer blows of his mighty message made kings tremble and the mighty quake. Yet we find this man discouraged. For six months he had languished in the dismal confines of Herod's prison without a visit or so much as a word from his Lord. With dwindling ardor he dispatched his attending disciples to inquire of this Man of Nazareth, "Art thou he that should come, or do we look for another?" Christ allowed John's messengers to examine His credentials: eyes for the blind; limbs for the lame; cleansing for the leper, hearing for the deaf; life for the dead. It was enough for the great baptizer. Without reluctance he accepted the high honor of making good his boast: "He must increase, but I must decrease."

Discouragement is ageless and universal. It visits the judge on the bench and the prisoner before him; the king in the palace and the beggar at his gate. Elijah made bold to defy four hundred and fifty prophets of Baal, but he couldn't avoid his juniper tree. Abraham, Moses, Peter, Paul — call the roll. No greater souls ever trod the highway of God's will, yet none of these escaped their moments of despondency.

Someone fancied that the devil had decided to go out of business and was selling his tools. Apart from the rest lay a wedge-shaped tool, much worn and priced higher than the others. It was called "discouragement." Asked why it was offered at such a price, the devil replied, "That is the most useful implement that I have. I've accomplished more for my cause with that tool than with all the rest combined." The story is fiction, but its truth is not. If Satan can cause us to lose heart, he is well on his way to hindering God's purpose for our lives.

Undeniably the Christian life is not without overhanging clouds and rocky roads beneath our feet. God hasn't deemed it wise to provide explanation for the adversities that beset us. Yet in the most trying hour we can know that He who marks the sparrow's flight and clothes the field-grass cares for us and conducts us in the way.

The precious promises of God's Word are the cure for discouragement. Each is like a bright star which penetrates the blackest night of despair. We read, "The steps of a good man are ordered by the Lord," and we are told, "All things work together for good to them that love God."

When I am discouraged I like to read Paul's writings and review the promise "Behold, I shew you a mystery; We shall not all sleep, but we shall all be changed." I like to think about the crown incorruptible that fadeth not away.

It cheers me to visit with John the Aged and hear him say again, "Beloved, now are we the sons of God

. . . but we know that, when he shall appear, we shall be like him."

And sometimes if the road is rough, I steal away to the Psalms where the Sweet Singer of Israel fills all the palace with the tuneful melody of voice and harp. I call to David: "Can God satisfy?" He strums his harp and makes reply: "The Lord is my shepherd: I shall not want."

"But the way is so difficult and the path so dreadfully steep!" Listen! "He maketh me to lie down in green pastures: he leadeth me beside the still waters. He restoreth my soul."

"But, David, there are wicked enemies. No one could know better than you the strength of the foe." "Thou preparest a table before me in the presence of mine enemies: thou anointest my head with oil; my cup runneth over."

"David, one of these days your nimble fingers will stiffen on the strings and those lips will mumble their last phrase. Your strong body will bend and sag, and with dim eye you will face the valley's gloom. In that sad hour will our God suffice?" Hear the glorious strains! "Yea, though I walk through the valley of the shadow of death, I will fear no evil: for thou art with me; thy rod and thy staff they comfort me."

What better cure for the disheartened? "Surely goodness and mercy shall follow me all the days of my life." When the last streak of light is seen in the west and earth has donned the shroud of everlasting night, when we climb to the top of Jacob's ladder and look back on sorrows that shall nevermore return, when we exchange this frail body for one immortal and perfect and awake in the image of Him whom we love and serve, we shall indeed be satisfied! Then shall we find rest from our toils in the shade of the tree of life and forget earthborne woes amid the murmurings of the crystal river that flows from the throne of God.

Discouragements will find an end, and like a day that is spent, be folded and laid away on the shelf of mortal history. But that happy day shall have no end. Eternal high noon! "I will dwell in the house of the Lord forever!"

# 17. THE REAL ENEMY

*Choose you this day . . .* (Josh. 24:15).

THE SCENE at Shechem was not peculiar to Joshua's day. It was the enactment of a drama as old as the human race and as young as today. It was the age-old story of human choice, whose principal characters are always the same — Almighty God, His prophet and the people. Yet had men eyes to probe the skies they might have beheld angelic hosts poised to watch on every battlement of heaven, so momentous is the significance of men's reaction to God's final warnings.

As today God's Word is God's voice, so in the days of Joshua did the prophet stand between God and the people to administer the ultimatums of heaven. It was the voice of the Almighty that day thundering across the summits and down the valleys; and when God speaks it always settles the question. Adam knew that as he beheld his nakedness and shame in Paradise lost. Pharaoh knew that as the Egyptians mourned their dead at midnight. King Saul knew that as he buried his sword in his wretched breast on the battlefield at Gilboa. "Choose you this day!" It was final then. It is final now.

Neglect is the most dastardly of all the enemies of mankind because of its unpretentious demeanor. It does not scowl menacingly or brandish a flaming sword. It wears a disarming smile. Yet its dagger drips with the blood of far more victims than does that of open infidelity and rebellion against God. It stabbed Pilate and damned his soul. Its sharp blade hewed down the mighty Felix and the august Agrippa. It was chief executioner in the wilderness as Moses implored the Israelites to look to the brazen serpent and live. Its vanquished lie sprawled grotesquely upon every page of history from the Egyptian Passover to the last Sunday service in your local church.

In a recent campaign I stood in a hotel lobby and heard a man curse God and defy Him openly. Such blatant arrogance shocks the most callous among us. Yet the man with burning oaths upon his unregenerate lips is not in a worse plight than he who says, "To-morrow!" Some souls steam full-speed over the precipice, whereas others simply drift to their doom. The tides of time will bring them to the same place. Indecision is not a vote for God, and Christ's words are decisive: "He that is not with me is against me."

Neglect never won a battle, or garnered a laurel, or erected a monument to fame. It doesn't plant, so it cannot reap. It doesn't attempt, so it cannot gain. It doesn't assail, so it cannot win. If Noah had waited to build the ark of safety, he would have perished in the flood. If Lot had hesitated to obey the angel's command to flee the gates of Sodom, he would have been consumed in the fires of destruction.

If the devil can get a man to postpone salvation, he is as sure of that man's soul as though the grave were already occupied and the judgment past. The human soul undergoes a hardening process as the years add themselves to a man, and woe to that one who awakes too late to the frightful fact that salvation's day is forever past and opportunity lies mutilated and dead in some frightful sepulcher. There is a tremendous note of urgency in the prophet's challenge, "Seek ye the Lord while he may be found." For too many it shall become the forerunner of the fateful assize, "Depart from me, ye cursed, into everlasting fire, prepared for the devil and his angels."

Open defiance toward God and wilful rejection of His terms of grace are not essential to man's damnation. Judas didn't bring down the lash on the naked back of Jesus: a Roman soldier did that. Judas didn't plait the crown of thorns that tore an ugly gash in His regal brow: the palace guards did that. Judas didn't nail Jesus to the Cross: other Jews did that. But the same hell that contains those whose spittle ran upon Christ's face contains Judas. He took the losing course. He chose merely to neglect the golden day of opportunity, and through that neglect forfeited eternal life.

How does God's warning read? "How shall we escape, if we . . ." Destroy the Bible? No! "How shall we escape, if we . . . " Demolish the church? No! "How shall we escape, if we . . ." Take up stones to slay the preacher? No! Hear God's reason for man's final and absolute destruction and flee from its terrible implications. "How shall we escape, if we *neglect* so great salvation?" That question has no answer!

To neglect salvation means doom, death, hell. There is no escape.

# 18. A WISHING WELL AND A MAGIC LAMP

*Ask what I shall give thee* (II Chron. 1:7).

THE STORY OF ALADDIN and his magic lamp is a fantasy well known to every schoolboy. Like all the tales of enchantment which concern wishing wells, fairy goddesses and magic wands, its attraction stems from its appeal to man's great yearning to have his air castles and daydreams become realities. According to the tale, the Chinese lad possessed a lamp which, when rubbed and wished upon, produced an enormous genie, a benefactor who was quick to grant the fondest ambition of its owner.

Who has not wished for such a wonderful lamp as this? Whose thinking has not been invaded from time to time by a desire to meet someone with power to honor a paramount choice and vouchsafe its utter fulfillment?

I do not say the Arabian story of Aladdin was borrowed. I do say it had a predecessor. The sacred record tells of Solomon, the son of David, who, shortly after his inauguration as king of Israel, was allowed a wish and was guaranteed its fruition. "In that night did God appear unto Solomon, and said unto him, Ask what I shall give thee." In one of the most dramatic of all incidents, secular or sacred, the young king made his choice. "Give me now wisdom and knowledge, that I may go out and come in before this people." Because of the magnificence of the demand, the Lord not only granted the desire but gave him unparalleled riches beside, so that Solomon is remembered as both the wisest and richest of men.

"Ask what I shall give thee." What a field day such a thought would bring to any mind! Not everyone would follow Solomon's example and ask for wisdom. To some the occasion would afford a golden key to inestimable possessions and fabulous wealth. Others would request fame, honor, perhaps power. There are those who would settle for a veneer of dazzling beauty; still others for a round of revelry and sensual pleasure with inexhaustible physical reserve to pursue it the longer. The hungry might wish for food; the naked for raiment; the sick for health; the weary for rest. What would your choice be?

Suppose you held Aladdin's lamp in your hand. Imagine that you were to be accorded one prime wish. God gave such an occasion to Solomon, and it is not unreasonable to believe that it might be repeated. What would you choose *if* you knew your wish would come true?

Erase the "if"!

The fact is, we *are* granted our wish! No one can deny that man's present and future are the result of his own choosing. His very life is a wishing well, and his moral will a magic lamp. As he passes through his valley of decision he finds he owns a mystical lantern which will summon a genie with authority to grant his wish. If the wish is evil, he will have the "god of this age" to do his bidding. If the choice be pure, he will find the "Giver of every good and perfect gift" ready to make his fondest dream come true.

In fact, man's entire history revolves around the wishing well. We are told that Enoch walked with God. He walked with God because he wished to do so. One day he saw the pathway growing golden beneath his feet and looked up into the glittering light of the eternal Eden. It happened according to his wish.

Did Daniel possess a magic lamp? In a sense he did. Like Abel, Noah, Abraham, Joseph, Moses and others, he found himself at the wishing well, and a choice lay before him. It was then that he purposed in his heart what his reward would be and set his course. His name today is a tower of strength and his future is glorious. All this once hinged upon a wish.

Once a man named Adam gazed into the wishing well and beheld a forbidden tree laden with tempting fruit. Rubbing the magic lamp of his inner will, he called forth his genie, demanded the fruit, and got it. Lot gazed into the same shimmering water and it wasn't long until he sat in the gate of Sodom, famous and wealthy. When Judas bent over the curb of the well, it was the thirty pieces of silver gleaming upon the sandy bottom that fascinated him. Quickly he made his choice; and almost as quickly he felt the smooth touch of silver in his greedy grasp. Man's wish comes true.

But something must be said concerning the two powers whose pleasure it is to make these dreams reality. Both are kings. Both have kingdoms out of whose store such grants are made. One, evil and crafty, stood in ancient times upon a hill, motioned to earth's kingdoms, and boasted, "All these things will I give thee, if thou wilt fall down and worship me." The other, holy and gracious, promises His own, "If ye shall ask anything in my name, I will do it." But the vital difference is in the fact that the one's reign is limited and his gifts only temporary, whereas the other's kingdom is eternal and His presents are from everlasting to everlasting. Adam, Lot, Judas and others found it out too late. In the light of the same truth shall the faithful of all ages eventually emerge victorious and triumphant.

Wait a minute! You're making a choice. That magic lamp in your bosom has power to gain you heaven or turn you hopelessly into hell. Your inviolate right to determine your own destiny, to walk with God or side with Satan, to go to reward or plunge toward retribution, demands that the utmost diligence be exercised. Your wish will last forever! Choose ye this day!

"Ask what I shall give thee." Man may so easily blunder in his choosing, crush his opportunity, and take a course of tragedy and doom. Or man may, on the other hand, select treasures in heaven where thieves steal not and moth and rust cannot corrupt. In the end he will find his destiny was settled at the wishing well. The great plan of the ages works that way.

# 19. DEATH

*For the wages of sin is death* (Rom. 6:23).

ORDINARILY A SERMON appearing under this title would be expected to deal with the Grim Reaper, whose all-consuming scythe has cut down those of every generation. This will be different. It views death as only a gruesome symbol of a worse condition among men everywhere. Earth is pocked with graves, and no city exists without its cemeteries, whose myriad tombstones remind the living of the dead. But we are not often enough made aware of a ghastly tragedy in which candles, shrouds and coffins play only a minor part. We fail to see that grim parade of the living dead who walk the streets of our cities, and move through our society to leave their ghost-like trail of human tragedy everywhere.

"She that liveth in pleasure is dead while she liveth." That is God's plain statement of fact. Paul, in building his framework of Christian theology, insisted that among non-Christians death is universal. He states definitely to the Romans, "Death passed upon all men, for that all have sinned." In this he speaks not of that death which blanches a human body and sends it back to the beggarly elements from whence it came. It is rather said concerning a frightful plague which buffets poor mortal man everywhere he goes — that death which settled over the earth like a hideous smog when Eden became the scene of man's transgressions and sin's awful consequence was seen to appear in every tangible possession of earth's domain.

The entire world is a tomb, and life is one long narrow "valley of the shadow." In this life man knows nothing save that which must pass away. He possesses only perishables. Not one thing endures. The processes of death are at work from center to circumference, making our planet an ugly revolving morgue of disintegration and decay. No matter what man clings to here, its end is frustration and total loss. That was King Solomon's mournful message in his book of Ecclesiastes when he sighed, "Vanity of vanities; all is vanity."

Unregenerate man exists on earth in a state of constant death, and all his properties are but the graveclothes of his vast sepulchral vault. He clings to money only to find that it tarnishes, corrodes and vanishes to leave him as penniless at his departure as when he first arrived. More often than not, its sordid touch dooms him to misery and shame, and when he faces the inevitable, provides only a box in which his flesh may putrefy. He sells his very soul for fame and position, both of which fade with the passing years as leaves fade with winter. He rises on a deceiving wave of popularity and sits in the seat of power until the immutable laws of degeneration splinter the throne beneath him and plunge him into the black abyss of obscurity. The glory which he knew at noon fades into the mocking silence of midnight, and he is forgotten. As beauty must vanish from the fair cheek of a maiden, and the baby's smile is not to be found on the withered lips of old age, so does the entire world wither. *Wither — and die.*

The dead are not all in the grave. Dead men often

join the laughing crowd, circulate in the streets, occupy seats of authority in human affairs. "You hath he quickened, who were dead in trespasses and sins," declared the apostle. "Let the dead bury their dead," demanded Christ. Christian theology assumes that men without Christ are estranged from God, and, as a mortal body is cut off from its quickening spirit, so these in their separation from God are morally and spiritually dead. Thus, when man by faith accepts the Lord Jesus Christ, he is known to have passed out of death and into life. "We know that we have passed from death unto life," was John's constant reminder to the early Christians.

Change and decay pervade the world, but this world is not our home. Here we have no sure resting place, no "continuing city," no lasting foundation. Our tabernacle is temporary and its entire setting unenduring. But the Christian seeks a better country. We journey toward a city which hath foundations whose builder and maker is God. For all those who are in Christ Jesus, death has passed away and all things have merged into the new life. Even the grave becomes an open portal to immortality.

All death shall some day have an end. Its viselike grip shall slacken, and its steel fingers shall grow limp. Disintegration shall cease, and deterioration shall prevail no longer. "Then cometh the end, when he shall have delivered up the kingdom to God, even the Father; when he shall have put down all rule and all authority and power. For he must reign, till he hath put all enemies under his feet. The last enemy that shall be destroyed is death." What a glorious truth! What a thrilling affirmation! It glistened beneath the pen of John the Aged when from Patmos Island he viewed the Everlasting City and wrote the gladsome tidings, "No more death!"

"For the wages of sin is death; but the gift of God is eternal life through Jesus Christ our Lord."

We wait the day when death shall be "swallowed up in victory."

# 20. THE GAMBLING RACKET

*When I have a convenient season, I will call for thee* (Acts 24:25).

Gambling is a racket which has never ceased to add impetus to the lawlessness and crime of every age. Organized gambling has discovered a weakness which exists in all mortal flesh and is out to cash in on it. Humans have an insane and persistent urge to gamble. It is an inborn something that has accompanied mankind from the beginning and has plagued his life and jeopardized his destiny. Gaudy cheating instruments in dimly-lighted casinos, widely-scattered smoke-filled bookie offices, even the more benign mediums of bingo, punchboards and raffles are but outward symptoms of a heart that "is deceitful above all things." Gambling deceives, hoodwinks, robs and destroys. Yet we gamble on.

The Bible has much to say about gambling and gamblers. I am not referring primarily to the type of gambling that took place at the foot of a cross when men set up their table of chance on the hallowed ground of Calvary and threw lots for the garments of the suffering Messiah. There is another form of gambling, more insidious and dangerous. The pawns are mortal life and the immortal soul, and heaven and hell are the stakes.

Concerning the origin of gambling we know little, save that it is older than the human race. We are told that in the dim and distant past a radiant angel, Lucifer, the sum of wisdom, and perfect in beauty, gambled for the throne of the universe upon the holy mountain of God. Today that impoverished seraph is called Satan and marks time in the prison house of darkness as he awaits final incarceration. Always, gambling leads to misery and despair.

In human history gambling is interwoven with the initial chapter. Adam, the first man, took a terrific chance on a soft and lenient God. His gambling paid off in counterfeit. When he left the weird shadow of the devil's gambling hall he found that he had forfeited his estate, his life and his soul.

Adam set an example from which his children have seldom deviated. He spawned a breed of gamblers who have infested every chapter of history and invaded all nations. Lot gambled from atop Mount Bethel, pitched his tent toward Sodom, and lost his sacred honor, his family and all his possessions. Samson gambled for pleasure in the home of Delilah and found himself deprived of both his strength and God. King Saul gambled for a few Amalekitish sheep and oxen, lost his throne and kingdom, and was discovered a bloody corpse on an alien battlefield. The roll call could go on and on. The cares of this world and the deceitfulness of riches have lured too many to disaster in sin's awful gaming house. Dives played there, a rich foolish farmer, a young ruler, Judas, Pilate, Demas, Agrippa, ad infinitum. These all gambled and lost.

The text that heads this message comes from the lips of a gambler. "When I have a convenient season, I will call for thee." Felix, for the sake of a vile woman and a high-ranking office, gambled with his soul that day. In this he was not alone. The greatest gambling racket in America is not necessarily being staged in the gambling halls of the land, and certainly does not attract the eye of the law. It is taking place in offices, schools, homes and even churches. It happens whenever and wherever men wager for continued opportunity and additional time. It happens when any man postpones the all-important matter of personal salvation through repentance toward God and faith in Jesus Christ.

Mortal man does not realize that God's great clock does not wait for procrastinators, sluggards, stragglers. Time keeps running out for deathless souls being weighed in eternity's balances. Judgment always strikes sooner than we think. There is not a man in hell who expected to be there. Those in hell are there because the unexpected happened. No one expects to die unsaved; to enter into eternity without being properly prepared to stand before God. We are numbed to approaching disaster; oblivious to impending doom!

God placed his great hour glass on the sill of heaven and told Noah to call his age to repentance. Some embellish their evangelistic sermons by declaring that the people scoffed and scorned the righteous man of God. I doubt such to be so. The Bible does not so teach. I have no doubt they were silenced by the godly life of this Ark-builder, appalled by his passion, deeply stirred by his message. But they took a chance. They waited. They gambled. And at last, amid the blinding lightning and deafening thunder, they perished.

Time ran out for the deluvians. Time ran out for

Sodom and Gomorrah. Time ran out for Belshazzar and his hosts. Hear the impassioned cry of the Saviour from the Mount of Olives as He looked down upon a hardened and indifferent nation: "O Jerusalem, Jerusalem, time is running out! The curtain is about to fall!" No wonder Jesus wept. No wonder He weeps today. The destruction wrought by Titus' armies upon the City of the Jews is the same judgment that will come swiftly to any nation that will not own the truth and make room for God.

Time is running out, America!

Time is running out for you, O man!

It is time to stop gambling and go to our knees to settle the mighty issues of our sins and God's salvation. The consequences of neglect and delay are too momentous to treat lightly. The accounting may come sooner and the judgment be closer than we think.

# 21. EARTH'S GREATEST PREACHER

*We trust we have a good conscience in all things*
(Heb. 13:18).

I AM THINKING JUST NOW of the greatest preacher of all time, outside of the Godhead.

He is a more noble pastor than Charles Haddon Spurgeon; a more capable evangelist than Dwight L. Moody; a more gifted expositor than John Wesley; a more effective reformer than Martin Luther; a more devoted saint than Augustine.

George Whitefields's open-air crowds often numbered more than ten thousand, but this preacher addresses millions.

Charles G. Finney's converts seldom strayed, so profound and lasting were the results of his labors, but the preacher to whom I refer far outranks Finney in the profundity and permanence of his work.

He belongs to no particular era or class or clime. He is as ageless as God, as impartial as grace, as universal as sin and salvation. His ministry began in the Garden of Eden. He was heard to cry out in protest at the spilling of the blood of righteous Abel. He preached in the household of Jacob, intruded into the secret chambers of David's palace, stood to accuse Judas and Pilate. His message and effectiveness have in no way diminished with the passing centuries that have stilled humbler voices and put lesser ambassadors in their graves.

I speak of Conscience.

His audience is limited only by the number of people who have been born. He has preached to all.

He does not confine his activities to pulpit and spire. He goes wherever man goes, and, in home and school, in field and forest, preaches everywhere.

He never tires or feels the need of rest. Not for thirty minutes or an hour, but every hour of the day and night his voice is heard in admonition, rebuke, counsel, encouragement, praise. He never pronounces the benediction. His sermons never end.

He is one preacher who will not be denied. His motive is to gain us heaven; but if resisted, he has the power to bring us down to hell.

Conscience, if properly treated, can be our best friend and greatest comfort. He cheered Joseph on the rocky bottom of a desert well. He made Daniel comfortable in the dungeon with a lion for a pillow and a lion's tail for a fan. He caused Paul to sing at midnight in a gloomy jail. He allowed Peter to sleep in his chains on the eve of his supposed execution. In this he is the minister of God to dispense peace and courage.

Conscience, if improperly treated, can be our worst foe and the cause of our greatest embarrassment.

Cain, taught by a father who had walked and talked with God, remained untouched by his family teachings; but the voice of Conscience heard in the field where lay the slaughtered Abel was so demanding as to make the murderer wail in the night that this punishment was more than he could bear.

Joseph, who swayed kings and ordered nations, could not persuade his brethren and received great injury at their hands; but Conscience invaded the scene, and at the invitation ten mourners cried aloud, "Verily, we are the guilty ones!"

Saul would not be moved by the sermons of Samuel; but Conscience tracked him down, and, commanding his two messengers, Memory and Remorse, drove a sword between his ribs and left him dead upon the field of battle.

Nathan could not order David's repentance until he opened the door to Conscience. A preacher greater than the prophet stepped into the council chamber, and before he left, the king of Israel was prostrate at the altar weeping for heaven's forgiveness.

Jesus, with miracle and parable, love and mercy, could not sway Judas. But Conscience found him in the night, turned the silver to acid in his palm, fitted a rope about his neck, pushed him over a cliff, dashing out his bowels on the rocks beneath.

Conscience is deathless. His ministry will not perish with the fleeting years or be dissolved when the passing ages melt into eternity. In hell, Conscience will set up his pulpit and preach to the damned. "Son, remember!" shall be his text, and he shall wield the lash of torment to be applied to every anguished soul who chose to fall into the hands of an angry God.

Taught by the Holy Spirit, directed by the Word of Almighty God, the preachments of Conscience are truth and his pronouncements binding. Let him have his way. No man has ever successfully resisted him.

# 22. SALVATION

*This day is salvation come to this house* (Luke 19:9).

I HAVE A DEEP SYMPATHY for the multiplied thousands whose names clutter the church records of our nation and who have achieved a "form of godliness" but have never discovered true salvation. There is no commodity known to mortal man which has been more grossly and consistently simulated than Christianity. Some go maliciously about their trade; we call them hypocrites. Others mistake a cheap imitation made up of ornate form and colorful ceremony for the genuine article, and belong to a class upon which Jesus once looked with compassion when He called them sheep without a shepherd. It is tragic when people who are blessed with much light and truth come short of rich Christian experience. Yet all the heathen are not confined to lands across the sea. America is full of them. They are people who become absorbed in a round of recitals, vested choirs, programs, chants and ritual — and have never found Jesus!

The nineteenth chapter of Luke's Gospel is the story of genuine salvation. It is the account of the Son of God seeking, finding and saving the lost! It is a story which incorporates every act in the drama of human redemption and reaches its grand climax in deep-wrought happiness and an absolutely changed life.

Zacchaeus' experience began where every real Christian's experience must begin: with a witness. "How shall they believe in him of whom they have not heard; and how shall they hear without a preacher?" Some have speculated that Bartimaeus, the blind beggar whose sight Jesus had restored on His way to Jericho, was the one who excited the little tax-collector to seek after the glorious One who now approached the city. Whether it was Bartimaeus or somebody else, Zacchaeus had been told, for it is written, "He sought to see Jesus who he was." The words form a fitting caption for the first chapter of the story.

He sought to see Him. The object of desire is important, but the intensity of that desire marks the difference between success and failure. Zacchaeus had every reason to despair, had he been seeking a predicate for defeat. He had a *moral* handicap, for he was a publican and had achieved his livelihood dishonestly. He had a *social* handicap, for he was rich, and Jesus said it was harder for a rich man to enter into heaven than for a camel to go through a needle's eye. Added to these was a *physical* handicap to impede his progress further. We read that he was small of stature and could not see Jesus because of the crowd that thronged Him. But the little man did not give up. He overcame his handicaps by running before the people and climbing into a sycamore tree. He knew Jesus would pass that way, and he was determined that nothing should hinder his getting a glimpse of Him.

What Zacchaeus lacked in legs he made up in will power. And after all, it isn't the length of the legs that counts, but how fast you can move them. A jack rabbit can outrun a horse if it wants to. The little Jew had set his mind to see Jesus, and soon his tenacity and sheer pluck had netted him a box seat at the performance. He got the best look of all!

"And Jesus entered and passed through Jericho." The long procession moved rapidly through the streets and came to a halt as Jesus reached the shade of the sycamore. And then it happened. The voice which once sounded upon the vacuum of space to produce a universe, the voice that more recently had stilled the storm, staunched disease, dispelled demons and summoned forth the dead, spoke once more: "Zacchaeus . . . come down; for today I must abide at thy house."

At this point many have forfeited the prize. The Son of God has spoken; the command has been given. Every eye shifts to the little Jew perched, halfhidden, among the leaves. Destiny hangs in the balance. A short while ago another had heard that voice and had turned about sorrowfully and departed because he had great possessions. Zacchaeus saw the richer gain, and losing sight of his earthly treasures in the light of the glorious grace of the incarnate God, "he made haste, and came down, and received him joyfully."

But the story does not end here. The strange silence is broken by another voice. It is that of the new convert: the voice of testimony. Lips are attesting to a miraculous transformation. Words of confession and restitution are heard: "Behold, Lord, the half of my goods I give to the poor; and if I have taken any thing from any man by false accusation, I restore him fourfold."

And Jesus said, "This day is salvation come to this house."

It is a simple story; the kind a child can read and understand.

But it is a story of true salvation.

# 23. A LESSON IN OPTOMETRY

*Except a man be born again, he cannot see . . .*
(John 3:3).

Here is an excerpt from a discourse that took place between the Master Eye Doctor of all time and one of His patients. All the symptoms focused in the complimentary conjecture which served only to expose a frightful malady: "We perceive that thou art a teacher come from God." Why did not Nicodemus behold in Jesus the incarnate One, the only begotten of the Father, Him in whom all fullness dwelt? Jesus answered that question when He said, "Except a man be born again, he cannot see . . . "

Nicodemus displayed the greatest measure of unregenerate vision. His material eyes, witnessing the mighty works of Christ, saw what the rankest sinner sees — a teacher come from God. Such insight has often given vent to high-sounding tributes, which, though they burden current literature with bouquets of verbal flattery, fail to afford that perfect attestation which Christ demands and deserves. The natural man beholds Jesus the teacher, Jesus the physician, Jesus the philosopher, and pronounces Him the "greatest man of all history." It is not enough to merely render acclaim. When spiritual eyes are opened to envision a spiritual world, one sees in Jesus Christ not simply a great teacher, but Him in whom all fullness dwells.

The vision of too many is confined simply to the

physical and moral characteristics of Christ. Carnal eyes fail to see the deeper motives of His ministry and the more vital truths of His Person. We espy His system of ethics, His philosophy of love; but we miss the fact that these cannot be practiced until we, through new birth, partake of His divine nature. We simply fail to see that the only way humanity will ever be brought to live the Sermon on the Mount is through regeneration by the Cross-work of the Christ of Calvary.

We must reckon with two worlds, one physical, the other spiritual. Through natural genesis we are able to appreciate air to breathe, food to eat, clothes to wear and a world of varied natural pleasures. But another world is introduced in Christ's assertion "My kingdom is not of this world." It is a world within men. It is a realm that consists of righteousness and peace and joy in the Holy Ghost. It is the kingdom of God. The only way one can comprehend the qualities of this kingdom is, as in the case of the physical world, to receive a birth into it. "But the natural man receiveth not the things of the Spirit of God: for they are foolishness unto him: neither can he know them, because they are spiritually discerned."

Imagine an unborn babe discoursing intelligently on the natural wonders of this physical world. Such a suggestion is foolish. Yet there are those who pose as authorities on spiritual matters who have never experienced a spiritual birth. They are blind leaders of the blind. As well might a babe who has never received origin recite the characteristics of Niagara Falls or the Grand Canyon or the Painted Desert. These have no stock and store out of which to discourse on the things of God. "Except a man be born again, he cannot see . . . "

After all, the full and final certification of this cardinal doctrine of the Christian faith is the experience itself. The new birth affords the only doorway to spiritual life and consequent spiritual discernment. In this respect we are reminded of the blind boy who had a delicate operation performed upon his eyes. When at last the operation had taken its course and the bandages were removed, he was led into a garden where his gaze fell upon bowers of roses, tall swaying cedars, beds of violets and daffodils and water lilies that floated in pools of azure blue. In utter delight he exclaimed to his mother, who stood close by, "Why didn't you tell me it was so beautiful?" To which his mother replied, "I tried to, my son, but you couldn't see; you were blind."

Youth is saying, "We cannot see what is wrong with the dance or similar conformity to the society in which we live." Parents are saying, "We cannot see the evil in social drinking and gambling if done in moderation." An untoward generation is saying, "We cannot see the need for the revival of repentance and conversion that some advocate." These diagnose their own case all too well—*they cannot see!* They are blind! Lying with the sightless at some modern Bethesda, they reach out to touch the halt and withered about them, and they compliment themselves that they do not share the desperate circumstances of others. But had they eyes to see the more distant horizon they would behold some David marching out to slay a Goliath; some Joshua's band en route to pull down the walls of a Jericho. God give us eyes that see the higher road, the more perfect standard, the more excellent way! God give us back that Christian experience that will establish us upon the plane of righteousness that exalts a nation!

The conditions of this Christ who said He came for the "recovering of sight to the blind" are ever and always, "Ye must be born again." Stephen heeded, and saw the Son of Man standing at the right hand of God. Paul heeded, and saw glories that could not be couched in human language. John heeded, and saw the New Jerusalem with its gates of pearl, its streets of gold, its crystal fountains. So may we, through belief in that One "lifted up," receive such vision as shall penetrate the shroud of this dying world and behold that day of grand consummation when we shall be like Him, "for we shall see him as he is."

# 24. A WORKING FAITH

*Not every one that sayeth . . . but he that doeth*
(Matt 7:21).

THE KEY to a full-orbed Christian experience combines two words which, in many Christian circles, are considered antipodes. It is supposed that such a deadly feud exists between faith and works that the two acts cannot possibly be reconciled. Entire systems of theology have been framed in defense of each to the veritable outlawing of the other, as though the one could not possibly survive where the other thrives.

One great failing of present-day orthodoxy is a persistent tendency on the part of isolated groups within the ranks to take an extreme stand on various controversial Bible subjects. The words of the Psalmist, "Forever, O Lord, Thy word is settled in heaven," form a paradoxical background for our diversity of interpretations. It is a joy to know that the Word is settled somewhere. A great victory will be scored for the cause of Christ when evangelical Christianity holds dogmatically to the great verities of salvation and then makes such conciliation on the nonessential, dubious issues as to create a common meeting place for us all. When that day comes it will be found that the real truth lay not at either extreme, but at a point near an equal distance from both.

The Bible declares that salvation is to be claimed by faith. The same Bible asserts that there is no salvation apart from works. Faith and works are not incompatible. The Book has joined them, and man had best not put them asunder. "Faith without works is dead."

Every true Bible believer, regardless of denomination, is bound to admit that salvation by human merit is an impossibility. The Scriptures leave no doubt at this point: "Not by works of righteousness which we have done, but according to his mercy." "It is the gift of God, not of works." But if salvation without faith is impossible, salvation without works is equally impossible. God's great gift is free, and is obtained without money and without price, but the Book is replete with reminders that saving faith is that which sprouts and blossoms and fruits in holy exercise. A careful study of the Word of God is enough to convince the student that simple belief is not saving faith. James discounts a fruitless, empty "believism" with this admonition: "Thou believest; Thou doest well: the devils also believe, and tremble." Those who heard Christ's Sermon on the Mount heard a similar rebuke: "Not every one that sayeth unto me, Lord, Lord, shall enter into the kingdom of heaven; but he that doeth the will of my Father which is in heaven." Christ demanded a working faith; nothing less!

Such was the faith of the early apostles. Their works did not save them, but the faith that brought them salvation was not without works. They believed, and forth from their inmost beings flowed rivers of living water. You will not find the soft, easy "just believe" doctrine in the book of Acts. We find that in those victorious days out of which we derive our lessons of polity and conduct, when a man "got religion" his religion "got him"! Salvation and service were counterparts of Christian experience. Christ's assertion "By their fruits ye shall know them" received its rightful meaning in their working faith.

"If any man will come after me, let him deny himself, and take up his cross daily, and follow me." Dare we lower the standard? Can the cost of Christianity be brought down, like that of a common commodity sold on the market, to where it may be offered to fakes and cheats at their own price? God forbid! Beheaded John, bloody Stephen, crucified Peter, a guillotine blade crimson with the blood of the Apostle Paul — these remind us that faith must not stand alone. These men professed. They did more: they *possessed!* The splendid testimony of their lips was exceeded only by the glorious testimony of their lives. Their faith was a light that shone before men, and men witnessed that light and glorified the Heavenly Father. Such is the working faith required of all who would enter into the kingdom. Not everyone that sayeth — but he that *doeth!*

# 25. JUST A THOUGHT!

*As he thinketh in his heart, so is he* (Prov. 23:7).

MODERN PSYCHOLOGY dresses an ancient truth in modern garments when it declares, "Thoughts running over the same mental track repeatedly, groove themselves to permanency." Psychology only reiterates a fact voiced centuries ago when Israel's king, under divine inspiration, said of man, "As he thinketh in his heart, so is he." Although the Bible is not primarily a book of science, it has always been found to be scientifically correct. History is itself proof of the compatibility of true science and the Scriptures. Scientific research has often sought out its own way, but invariably it finds that its way finally converges with the ways of God, whose ways are of old, changeless and everlasting.

Every thought we think leaves its impression on the cortex (the thinking matter) of the brain. If we think the same thought twice, the impression becomes more pronounced. If we think the same thought constantly, the impression becomes a veritable rut, and it becomes increasingly difficult to reroute our thinking.

A recent issue of *Reader's Digest* told of a detour sign which read, "Choose well your rut; you're going to be in it a long time." This startling statement of fact might well be applied to our thinking. Vehicles traveling over a dirt road for the first time leave scarcely a trace of their having passed that way; but during the course of years they wear away the earth until the road is rutted and the wheels confined to grooves of their own making. Our stream of thought, like the churning waters of the Colorado through the Grand Canyon, digs away at the strata of nerve tissue until a mighty chasm with insurmountable walls is fashioned to hold the thought captive. As a man at first is master of his thought, so, at last, the thought becomes master of the man.

Men are molded by their thoughts. Big ideas make big men; shallow thinking results in shallow character. It is said that during his early years David Livingstone had a large map of Africa on his bedroom wall. Africa became his very life long before he became a missionary and, in quest of the lost, lived and died in the tangled jungles of that land. Livingstone's heart has long since mingled with the elements of that Dark Continent where at first only his thinking provided a bridge over which he traveled to make it his world. Where man's treasure is, there will his heart be also.

There was never a man who reached the giddy heights of genuine success who was not driven there by a dominating thought. Luther was compelled to champion the Reformation by the captivating idea, "The just shall live by faith." Wesley drew two continents closer to heaven with the forceful conviction that Christianity cannot exist apart from a personal experience of salvation in Jesus Christ. Sam Jones, the South's great evangelist, attributed his success to the fact that he had been overpowered by the belief that the preacher is not a hired man of the people but an ambassador for Almighty God.

God's warning that a man's thoughts and his character are inseparable may be observed on the seamy side of life. In talking with derelicts and outcasts I have seen this truth at work. Once I asked a railroad tramp to tell me about the biggest idea he ever had. He scratched his dirty beard and replied, "Bud, I don't think I ever had one!" I've talked to convicts and felons and those who pursue illicit practices and have found that a thought of lewdness or lawlessness, at first their brain child, grew to Frankenstein proportions within them and drove them to commit their godless crimes. The Bible is correct. Thoughts make men!

Small wonder Paul exhorts, "Whatsoever things are true, whatsoever things are honest, whatsoever things are just, whatsoever things are pure, whatsoever things are lovely, whatsoever things are of good report; if there be any virtue, and if there be any praise, think on these things."

Have you discovered the value of right thinking? Banished Cain, disgraced Lot, sightless Samson, pitiable Saul, murdered Haman, remorseful Judas, frustrated Pilate — all bear testimony to the fact that a man's thoughts may prove his embarrassment. Honored Abel, favored Abraham, exalted Joseph, victorious Joshua, renowned Daniel, the famed eleven, immortal Paul lend as strong a tribute to the fact that a man's thoughts may prove his highest virtue.

Turn your eyes toward early Christianity to discover the secret of its virility and strength in those days when the infant Church was making inroads into every stronghold of evil in city, province, state and nation. Out of those glorious years came the admonition of an early advocate: "If ye then be risen with Christ, seek those things which are above, where Christ sitteth on the right hand of God. Set your affection on things above, not on things on the earth." The oracle's appeal is imperative. True Christianity can never be divorced from spiritual affections.

The relationship of a man's soul to God is best evidenced by those things which get that man's attention. "As he thinketh in his heart, so is he!"

# 26. THE GOOD OLD DAYS

*Return unto me, and I will return unto you*
(Mal. 3:7).

IN TRAVELING throughout most of the forty-eight states as I bear the Gospel tidings, I repeatedly come in contact with people who are living in the yesteryears. Even folk who have the forward look cannot refrain from occasionally looking backward. And as they gaze wistfully upon bygone times, they sigh with deep longing, "Ah, but those were the good old days!"

I have found entire cities that were devoted to the backward look. Ask any citizen of Springfield, Illinois, about Abe Lincoln, and you'd better be prepared to kill an hour on the spot! Boston maintains that she is progressive, but I found her still taking time to dust the ancient pews of old North Church!

If the South does not exceed the North in commerce and industry, she certainly puts her to shame in reliving the glorious past. Visit any village square, turn almost any bend in the road, and you have a rebel soldier bearing down on you with gleaming bayonet. Of course, he's a bit stiff and cold and rather old. You see, he's made of bronze. But the look of determination is in his face, and the proud set of his jaw harks back to a golden day of Southern aristocracy which the people are loath to forget. His metallic heart beats to the rhythm of "Auld Lang Syne" while the creaking of antique rockers heard near by and the glow of old brass lamps in the windows present a fitting atmosphere for precious memory. Who will deny that those were grand old days? Somehow they still attract us, and beckon us to return.

I'm still a young man, but I must confess that I have already been guilty in my solitude of reciting the lines of the sentimentalist:

> Backward, turn backward,
> O Time in your flight,
> And make me a child again
> Just for tonight!

Strange how we spend the first years of our lives wishing we'd grow old and the last looking covetously back upon the times when we were young. Yet this practice is broader than the individual, and often crops out in a local "Pioneer Days" celebration or a national "Freedom Train." Something in human nature makes a man enjoy reminiscing. If you don't believe me, go to the corner store on Saturday night or walk through Pershing Square on a Sunday afternoon. It's the topic of conversation — the good old days!

Some of you will remember them. I speak of those days when I was still trying to swing a passport to my native Texas. But I've heard tell! I hear there was a time when people prayed out of their hearts instead of from a mimeographed sheet. I hear there was a day when preachers hadn't yet discovered the convenience of prying their sermons out of cloth-bound "cans," but, instead, preached the pure Word of God and thrilled their hearers with sure-enough Gospel. I hear there was a day when our churches were so filled with the glow of the dazzling Light of the world that there was no need for flickering candles and lighted crosses to get the people "in the mood."

Those were the days of great spiritual revivals; days when the Gospel itself was stronger than all the altar "tricks" that could be mustered by evangelists; days when God came down men's souls to meet, and glory crowned the mercy seat! Those were the days when the Bible was held to be full and final authority in all matters of Christian doctrine; when the virgin birth and deity of our Lord went unquestioned; when the blood of the Cross still cleansed from sin and the Gospel of Christ was still the power of God unto salvation.

Since that day the Christ-haters and Bible-debunkers have swarmed in from their hideouts to make merciless attack on all that once combined to make America the greatest nation on earth. They have thrown the Bible out of our public schools. They have scorned religious revivals. They have ridiculed the Christian home and scoffed at the family altar. They have infiltrated our pulpits to water down the mighty message of blood-bought redemption and have stuffed our Lord Jesus Christ into a human mold. Their poison has reached the seats of government until our very leaders are afraid to pray.

Since that day we have suffered the wages of our folly. Our churches are cold on Sunday morning, blacked out on Sunday night, echo in their emptiness at the midweek prayer hour. Our nation is steeped in sin, with the women outrunning the men to pluck the bitter fruits of their infidelity. The general trend of America is in the direction of Sodom and Gomorrah!

Since that day the earth has twice been bathed in

blood, and the awful horror of two world wars is crowded from our memory by the hovering clouds of a third which threatens to send the curtain crashing down on civilization itself. All our elaborate schemes and systems for a universal peace have disintegrated before our eyes like a castle of sand. The United Nations has shown itself to be a record of failures.

Somehow out of the chaos and confusion of it all there seems to come the faint echo of a voice that has long been lost in the rabble and riot of our modern paganism. It is the voice of the Saviour still pleading, "Return unto me, and I will return unto you . . . And all nations shall call you blessed: for ye shall be a delightsome land."

Let's go back to the good old days!

# 27. BACK FROM THE DEAD

*You hath he quickened, who were dead* (Eph. 2:1).

PAUL IS NOT WRITING to Lazarus of Bethany, whose deceased body Christ raised from the dead. He is not directing his words to Jairus' daughter, whom the Lord brought back to life in Jerusalem. He does not address himself to the widow's son, whose funeral procession Jesus broke up with a resurrection at Nain. He writes in the Ephesian letter to people who never suffered the cramped quarters of a coffin or endured the musty confines of a tomb. Yet he writes to those "who were dead."

It is a tragic fact that a host of preachers today are ignoring one of the greatest fundamentals of the Christian faith. A large percentage of American ministers have substituted the preaching of character for the essential message of regeneration. As well ask a rotting corpse to love God and treat his neighbor kindly as to ask an unregenerate man to pattern after the character of Christ. There can be no Christian character until there is Christian nature; and there can be no Christian nature until there is new birth.

"You hath he quickened." The word "quickened" means "made alive." The current theory upon which many pastors base their message, that men bear the image of God and need only to have that image developed, has no Scriptural foundation. In Genesis we read that God created Adam in His own image. But in pursuing the account we find sin knocking at the door, and Adam opening to the Tempter. When sin came in, the image of God went out. Adam fell, and in falling forfeited the image of his Creator, which image cannot associate with sin. We read further that Adam knew his wife and that she bore him a son whose name was Cain. Cain was not born in the image of God, but in the image of fallen Adam, and his act of murdering his brother Abel proved it. From that day to this, men have been born physically alive but spiritually dead. Man can regain the image of God and consider himself a member of the divine family only by undergoing a new birth. It is through spiritual regeneration that we "who were dead" are "quickened."

The man is in error who thinks he can live to please God without spiritual regeneration. "They that are in the flesh cannot please God" is the Bible's settling of that question. Jesus warned Nicodemus that no man could understand the things of God until he was born again. The earth is geologically understood. The solar system is astronomically understood. A cathedral is architecturally understood. An automobile is mechanically understood. The kingdom of God is spiritually understood. Until we attain unto spiritual life there can be no spiritual understanding. Until such experience is ours there can be no spiritual discernment. Ye must be born again.

Those who renege at the threshold of Christianity because there is so much mystery involved are indeed inconsistent and unfair. Why should religion be singled out and treated as no other subject? Because we cannot explain every detail of electricity, do we therefore abolish its use? Because we cannot explain fully the intricacies of digestion, do we therefore stop eating? Because respiration is mysterious, do we outlaw breathing? Yet some people, because they cannot comprehend some one factor of Christianity, foolishly, and to their eternal peril, reject the entire system.

These same people enjoy a thousand phenomena which they have never even attempted to explain. They enjoy physical life, yet no one has ever offered a satisfactory explanation for life. They think, yet thought and memory are among the deepest of mysteries. They cannot explain emotion, yet they do not hesitate to weep and laugh and love. They cannot fathom the laws of gravity, inertia and centrifugal force, yet they constantly respect and utilize these inexplicable laws.

Let the reasoner who will not accept the new birth because of its mystery explain the laughing babe, the warbling bird, the nodding flower. Let him explain how that stagnant swamp became a fleecy cloud which descended like a veil of angel's tears upon the mountain, to go dancing through the ravine and tumbling over the canyon wall like a ribbon of sliding moonlight to find the sea. Let him explain how the sluggish clod is transformed into the fair form and comely features of a pretty maid; or how the senseless sod takes on the velvet hue of the violet, spins a verdant robe about its fragile form, and touches its lips with a perfume that saturates every zephyr that bends to kiss it in its floral paradise. Let him explain how the sky-blue egg in the bough becomes the delicate structures of the feathered chorister whose music at eventide is softer than the touch of dew and sweeter than the vesper chimes.

"You hath he quickened, who were dead." Explain it? God never intended that we should. Enjoy it? For centuries untold millions have, and so may you! The power to transform still belongs to Him who, in the beginning, fashioned our first parents from earthly elements and gave them the breath of human life. And in the hearts of countless millions, themselves the prime proof of the experience, still rings the glorious promise, "To as many as received him, to them gave he power to *become* the sons of God."

# 28. THE CUP

*The cup which my Father hath given me, shall I not drink it?* (John 18:11).

IT IS A VITAL FACT that in recording the Gethsemane scene of Christ's passion all four evangelists give a significant place to the mention of a cup. The combined accounts present the following sequence:

> And he took with him Peter and the two sons of Zebedee . . . And they came to a place which was named Gethsemane . . . and [Jesus] began to be sorrowful and very heavy . . . And he went a little farther, and fell on his face, and prayed, saying, O my Father, if it be possible, let this cup pass from me: nevertheless not as I will, but as thou wilt . . . He went away again the second time, and prayed, saying, O my Father, if this cup may not pass away from me, except I drink it, thy will be done . . . And being in an agony he prayed more earnestly: and his sweat was as it were great drops of blood falling down to the ground . . . And he prayed the third time, saying the same words . . . Then said Jesus unto Peter, put up thy sword into the sheath: the cup which my Father hath given me, shall I not drink it?

Herein lies a mystery as vast as that which surrounds the Incarnation, as deep as that which blankets the dark hours when the Calvary Lamb cried out in infinite loneliness, "My God, my God, why hast thou forsaken me?" That God should be found in an earthly garden is wonder enough; that He should be discovered in the throes of conflict over a cup is unfathomable! He whose hands once formed the stars and fashioned the pattern of the nebulae now holds a cup. He whose eyes first reflected the glitter of a sun and watched the fiery trail of the comet through boundless space looks with dread upon a cup. He whose mind, in the dim recesses of eternity, conceived a universe and calculated a plan for the ages now shrinks from a cup. He who existed before Abraham, and at whose feet someday every knee shall bow, treads the winepress alone, and groans from the depths of bitterest woe, "Father, if it be possible, take this cup away!"

Finite reasoning cannot fully comprehend the occasion. Fleshly eyes would fail to discover the awful spectacle of the cup of that crisis hour, when the sweat of the suffering Messiah ran crimson down his brow and the soul of the Only Begotten was "sorrowful, even unto death." The eyes of Christ were not limited, nor was His mind the stunted mind of mortal, so that the terrifying impact of the contents should escape detection. As others slept close by, He watched. And as He watched, a sinner spat out blasphemy — and it settled in the cup. A lustful rascal desecrated a woman's virtue — and it reached the cup. A drunken son strangled a tender mother — and murder made its way to the cup. A depraved degenerate snatched a wee babe from its mother's arms and dashed its brains out on the rocks — and depravity was in the cup. Every deed of nameless wrong hatched in the black haunts of hell, every smear of debauchery and stain of iniquity, settled like thick, black dregs to the bottom of the cup.

The Sinless One drew back. His flawless character revolted. The wheels of redemption stood still as Jesus, with trembling fingers, raised the cup. His garments were now gory in the sweat of His soul-agony, and the slumbering disciples aroused to hear only the plea, "Father, if it be possible, let this cup pass from me!"

Do we have the entire prayer He prayed in that dark hour? Ask the olive trees; they say He moaned, "Father, I have never sinned! I have never tasted of forbidden fruit!" Ask the rolling hills; they say He pleaded, "My character is unstained, unsullied, untarnished; I am holy as Thou art holy!" Ask the rugged rocks; they say he cried aloud, "O Father, must I who am without spot drain the dregs of this cup so polluted and vile? Must I who am sinless become sin?" Was this His prayer? Someday beyond this vale of imperfection we shall know. For now it suffices to say that He had come to learn the Father's will, and when it was made known to Him, He turned to one whose dull understanding failed to take in the greater glory of the hour and said, "Put up thy sword into the sheath: the cup which my Father hath given me, shall I not drink it?"

O the magnificence of it all! Earth, hide yourself in shame among the constellations! Stars of heaven, blush as you run to put on mourning! Little man, throw yourself in embarrassment into the dust from which you came! How undeserving all! Heaven has stooped to earth in mercy. The God-man has pressed the cup to His lips and its bitter contents slip away. He who knew no sin has become sin for us, that we might become the righteousness of God in Him.

And so He leaves the garden in full victory. The light of triumph is upon His brow. There is no terror now. Caiaphas' court presents no fear. Pilate's judgment hall can hold no alarm. The scourge, the spittle, the thorns, the nails, the spear were in the cup. The Cross was in the cup. And Jesus drank the cup.

Hallelujah! What a Saviour!

# 29. A GREAT MAN'S BOAST

*But God forbid that I should glory, save in the cross* (Gal. 6:14).

PAUL THE APOSTLE had much of which to be proud. His background was superb. The rich blood of aristocracy surged through his noble veins. He traced his lineage to the tribe of Benjamin, of the stock from whence came Mary, the mother of Christ. His early record was phenomenal. Jerusalem owned seventy-one outstanding citizens who comprised the Sanhedrin. Paul, before his conversion, had been their mouthpiece. It was he who, with a zeal that far outstripped that of the most conscientious scribe, carried the exploits of the Jewish council into every surrounding territory. Truly he was a Pharisee of the Pharisees!

Paul's conversion was spectacular. He might have boasted the only experience of its kind, for Christ left His priestly duties in heaven long enough to deal with him personally on the Damascus Road. The ministry into which he immediately launched was unmatched among the apostles. In churches established, in cities visited and countries invaded, in converts gained, he excelled them all. Half the epistles in the New Testament came from his pen. It was largely through his influence that the infant Church became the mighty force that broke the power of Rome. He gave the Church its first theology and established a form for Church administration that is without equal today. Surely Paul might justly have boasted of the tremendous success that attended his preaching of the Glad Tidings.

Nor did opportunity for boasting end here. The eleventh chapter of the second Corinthian letter gives us another picture of the man. "In labours more abundant, in stripes above measure, in prisons more frequent, in deaths oft. Of the Jews five times received I forty stripes save one. Thrice was I beaten with rods, once was I stoned, thrice I suffered shipwreck, a night and a day I have been in the deep." Who would despise such a record of merit achieved in the line of Christian duty?

Undoubtedly Paul represents a high watermark in Christian endeavor since the day of Christ. No other conversion compares with the glory of his; no other consecration was more sure or victory more complete; no other testimony was brighter or ministry more abundant. Yet we observe him in the text, possessed of the same humility that accompanied his only autobiography, "Chief of sinners." Gathering all his trophies and triumphs together, he laid them at Jesus' feet and retained but one all-consuming boast — "But God forbid that I should glory, save in the cross!"

To the apostle, the Cross of Calvary was far more than a symbol of execution. The death of Christ was more than an episode of martyrdom. Paul saw in the Cross, Heaven's sacrificial altar, the altar upon which God's Lamb was slain for the sins of the world. Here was the focal point of salvation; the foundation upon which the wheels of redemption moved.

He gloried in that Cross because in its very essence he observed the true nature of God. Not the lush, easy God of the moderns, but the God of perfection and holiness, whose fundamental righteousness would not waive the penalty of sin, though it cost Him His Son that He might be "just, and the justifier" of all who believe.

He gloried in the Cross because he found there his conception of Christ. Not the Christ of the humanist, emasculated and limited to mere human exploits, but the Christ of creation, the source of light, the author of life and sole administrator of salvation.

Paul gloried in the Cross because it reflected the truest picture of himself. Certainly the very fact of God's demand for just recompense and the fact of Christ's dying were proof enough of man's depravity and total inability to save himself. Standing before its scenes, Paul found his message, and turning to a dying world, he declared, "I determined not to know any thing among you, save Jesus Christ, and him crucified!"

Oh, the glory of the Cross! Like a mighty derrick lifting its strong structures over cool water, it beckons to the Well of Salvation. It is earth's only contact with heaven; man's only approach to God. It is the only vent of blessing, pouring forth from the riven heart of the Saviour. Answering every claim of justice, it becomes the sole medium of mercy, and man can only stand abashed within its shadow to echo the mighty weight of a great man's only boast.

> In the Cross of Christ I glory,
> Tow'ring o'er the wrecks of time;
> All the light of sacred story
> Gathers round its head sublime.

# 30. THE VIRGIN BIRTH

*Behold, a virgin shall conceive, and bear a son, and shall call his name Immanuel* (Isa. 7:14).

It is doubtful that Isaiah consulted the educationalists of his day before he recorded this unusual prophecy. He probably did not so much as counsel with even one scientist to ascertain the "scientific probability" of his revelation. Nor is it likely that he was greatly affected by the torrid stream of criticism that must have splashed from the sulphur-scented laboratories of the biologists. Had not God spoken? Had not the word of the Spirit been plain? His duty was not to debate, nor even to defend, but to declare! And so he wrote it — "Behold, a virgin shall conceive, and bear a son."

To Isaiah nothing was impossible with the God who had created all things and whose immutable counsel controlled the swift stars in their courses and the raging seas within their boundaries. The marvel was not the virgin birth, but the fact that God had condescended to send His Son into this sinful, shameful world at all. That He was to be conceived in the womb of a virgin by the Holy Ghost was no more to be doubted than that the sea had divided before the lifted rod of Moses, or that the sun had stood still for the armies of Joshua. Seemingly the prophet had not taken membership with that clique of divines who feel they must limit God to the normal and allow Him credit only for those things produced by natural order. The miracle of a bird in the air, a fish in the sea, a flower in the sod, the miracle of a babe nestled to its mother's breast was too much for his poor mind to comprehend. Why should he question the ability of the God who made the first Adam, with neither father nor mother, to present the last Adam to the world without a father? There was not the slightest qualm as he added another miracle to the grand category and wrote, "A virgin shall conceive."

The spirit of Isaiah seems lacking in the hearts of some who have currently brought this cardinal doctrine under withering attack. Within the camp there have arisen some self-styled Nadabs and Abihus to offer strange fire before the Lord and to declare that a belief in the virgin birth of Christ bespeaks neither a sound mind nor a well-framed theology. The pity is that their advocacy of accepting only that which has physical explanation simply cannot be made to stop at this point. Their unbelief eats like acid at the very vitals of Christianity. It becomes a wild horseman with bloody spurs galloping over every sacred verity, plunging the lance deep into the heart of every fundamental. Like a hideous denizen of hell it rips from our Lord the robes of deity and makes His Calvary blood as impotent as water. It drags His resurrected, glorified and ascended body from heaven's throne and casts it back into the grave to rot with its fellows. It presents a heavenly holy of holies with neither a high priest nor the blood of remission, and grants Almighty God no suitable grounds upon which to justify a world of sinners. For their "intellectual pride" they barter the very Gospel. And while they sip their simmering pottage from the kettle of intellectual conceit, empty pews, barren altars, broken homes, crowded taverns and a corpulent crime list tell the ghastly story of a nation that has been betrayed.

To say that the virgin birth is not a doctrine essential to the Christian system of theology is no slight charge. Such an assumption challenges the very veracity of God's Word, which declares, "Now the birth of Jesus Christ was on this wise: when his mother Mary was espoused to Joseph, before they came together, she was found with child of the Holy Ghost" (Matt. 1:18). It ignores Christ's claims of pre-existence (John 17:5), of e-quality with God (John 14:9), of deity and Lordship (Matt. 22:43-45). It would give Him natural origin, thus depriving Him of power to forgive sins (Luke 7:48), ability to provide, by His substitutionary death, a ransom for the sins of all mankind (I Tim. 2:6), the right to grant resurrection and eternal life to all who believe (John 11:25-26).

Those who declare that one may become a Christian and disbelieve the virgin birth tread on dangerous ground. No one can be saved without belief in and obedience to the documentary declarations that pertain to the life, death and resurrection of the Son of God. These documents constitute our Bible, and the Bible certainly is not silent on this point. Paul speaks of Jesus in the following manner: "Who, being in the form of God, thought it not robbery to be equal with God: but made himself of no reputation, and took upon him the form of a servant, and was made in the likeness of men." To say that faith in this fact is not necessary to salvation is to say that Christianity does not demand faith in a divine Christ at all! We insist, with many outstanding scholars, that a belief in the virgin birth of our Lord is as vital to Christian experience as belief in the blood atonement and the willingness of God to save through that blood all who repent and believe.

Jesus Christ was virgin born. The Bible declaration, oft repeated, makes it so. When the Holy Ghost planted the seed of deity within the womb of the Virgin Mary and Jesus came forth, He was the incarnate God. He who had been from the beginning without a mother was transcended into time without a father. For "he is before all things, and by him all things consist." The mind that amazed the doctors when our Lord was twelve had, in the dim aeons of eternity, conceived the universe. The feet that walked the winepress alone once paced the illimitable space as omnipotence spake creation into being. The hands that clutched the blood-stained nails of a cross placed the iron in the hills and planted the forests from which were hewn the rough beams that lifted Him to shame. The lips that cried out in the darkness, "It is finished," once before cried out in darkness, "Let there be light," and there was light. With sixteen titles and unnumbered tributes the Bible ascribes deity to Him. Indeed, He is "the mighty God, the everlasting Father, the Prince of Peace"!

Let the apostles of apostasy stop at Jesus the man. We have discovered the pearl of greater price! "For in him dwelleth all the fullness of the Godhead bodily."

# 31. THE CHANGELESS FOR A CHANGING WORLD

*The immutability of his counsel . . .* (Heb. 6:17).

Ours is a world of change. Mountains rising from the deep but balance those that crumble to the plain. The hungry ocean nibbles at the beach while its tributaries dig into the valleys to supply the loss. The seasons constantly present new fashions. Winter with its cloak of ice will melt into the gushing streams of spring; and summer, drenched in golden warmth, will bear its various offspring for autumn to cover with a blanket of tinted leaves. Nature cannot be still. Like its impatient child, the restless sea, it tosses within its boundaries, presenting a varied countenance for each new day that bespeaks the mutability of all that it contains.

The changing world contains a changing people. Society is shifting, with philosophies and systems that drift unanchored to join those of the ancients which lie shattered on the barren shores of history. Man himself, the supreme creation of God's hand, is marked for deterioration and decay. His baby cry gives way to boyish shout, and soon his years are such that he stands the peer of some choice trade. He speaks, perhaps, a word heard round the world; or he may tease a secret from the atom; or yet may lead an army to enlarge his name. But always he is destined to return to the silent halls of oblivion. His eye grows dim, his ear dull, his back bent, his step feeble, and ere long he topples into the sod from whence he came, to lose identity in the nodding grass and swaying forest.

But change is not confined to the physical kingdom. It is a thieving force that invades the moral and spiritual realms for plunder never consigned to it. " 'To dust returneth' was not spoken of the soul!" Yet our dangerous age is characterized by a faltering faith accompanied by crumbling convictions and corrupt character which threaten with calamity the very fiber of the soul of man. It is not enough to say that our moral feet have slipped from the rock of truth and that we are sinking helplessly into the quicksands of international uncertainty. It is not enough to confess that our scientific brain children have turned upon us to press a dagger near our hearts, while our dream of "one world" merges into a ghastly nightmare of broken peace pacts, international betrayals and a steadily mounting certainty of global war. The tragic fact is that we, a people singularly blessed of God, have given away our heritage. We have forfeited the immutable counsel of God and have tightened our grasp upon the cheap ladle that holds the watery pottage of "sin for a season." We have gained the hollow thrill of lasciviousness only to find that it is costing us our birthright in democratic principles and those holy ideals that made for peace and safety and power in our yesteryears. Small wonder the multitudes, groping in the shadows, cry aloud, "Watchman, what of the night?" Will we point those who look to us for succor to another blind corridor in the labyrinth of human ingenuity, or will we dare to direct them to the sure foundation of the eternal Gospel with which our forefathers challenged a changing world with the unchanging verities of heaven?

Science records that the body of man undergoes a complete change in substance every seven years. But the heart of man has not changed. "Deceitful above all things, and desperately wicked," it still comes under the unalterable counsel of God: "There is no difference: for all have sinned and . . . the wages of sin is death."

Society's diary has not two pages the same in the nineteen hundred years that have passed since a Pharisee met with Jesus in the dim light of a street lamp, but the counsel of the incarnate God remains constant: "Ye must be born again!"

Men and nations have met to quaff their cup of life and sing their song of joy or woe only to crowd further that universal kingdom beneath earth's crust where there is neither king nor slave; yet the provision of God has neither aged nor perished.

"As many as received him, to them gave he power to become the sons of God."

As of old, every good and perfect gift can come only "from above, and cometh down from the Father of lights, with whom is no variableness, neither shadow of turning." And the only Saviour who can satisfy is God's Son, "the same yesterday, today, and forever."

We have discovered new ways, but have found them perishable ways in a perishing world. The right way is still the old way — the Calvary way. It is the way that leads to the fulfillment of every longing desire of our troubled hearts. We will find along that way the hope and content our fathers owned when they looked by faith toward an eternal day and an unchanging city. Surely it is time to join in their song, and claiming the changeless for this changing world, sing:

> Change and decay in all around I see;
> Oh, Thou who changest not, abide with me!

# 32. YESTERDAY, TODAY AND FOREVER

*He went away sorrowful* (Matt. 19:22).
*Soul . . . eat, drink, and be merry* (Luke 12:19).
*And in hell he lift up his eyes, being in torments* (Luke 16:23).

THE SPIRIT has manipulated the sacred camera to reproduce three likenesses for the gallery of history. To say that they portray an actual sequence in a single life would be presumption. That they represent the trend and destiny of any soul that will not own Christ is certain.

How expertly does the Divine Photographer catch the first phase of the insurgent life! Possessing every qualification that makes for worldly success yet lacking "that one thing" which spells security, a young man finds himself in the Valley of Decision.

Enthusiastically' he comes; sincerely he inquires; attentively he listens. How blessedly hopeful! Proudly he considers; stubbornly he resists; sadly he turns away. How utterly tragic!

As the eternal voices for good and ill vie for his soul, Mercy knocks in vain, Truth pleads to no avail, Conscience lifts imploring hands only to be struck down and trampled beneath rebel feet; and the die is cast!

"He went away sorrowful." The glistening tear, the ashen cheek, the trembling lip betray his composure and speak a language that false lips would never speak.

They say his heart is broken as he leaves the high noon of opportunity for the midnight of oppression. They say his soul is aching as he departs the source of salvation and enters the snare of Satan. They say his wounded character moans in anguish as he turns his back on the heights of holiness and his face toward the horrors of hell. Forsaking the only hand of healing, the only voice of verity, the only law of life, he stumbles blindly into the deepening night, clutching to his bosom not the Saviour — but his silver! That which once he possessed at last possesses him, and the slave must do the bidding of his chief. His possessions, dominating, leave no room for another master, and so he turns away. How many might occupy the place of the young man in the picture that we shall here entitle "Yesterday"! Well has the poet written:

> Still as of old
> Man of himself is priced:
> For paltry silver he still sells
> Himself, not Christ!

But we must go on, and as we stand before the next likeness the scene has changed. The choice of yesterday has blossomed into fruitage, and the god of this age has showered choice bounties upon his devotee. Money has multipled. Fame is fabulous. Position is peerless. As he views his padded pantry and bulging barns he laughs at the seeming folly of his sorrow on that sad yesterday when he decided in favor of earth's treasures. Hear his careless song resound down the hallways of his ornate mansion, "Soul, thou hast much goods laid up for many years . . . eat, drink, and be merry!" Poor fool! He does not realize that the game is never over until the last quarter is played, nor is the book finished until the final chapter is completed. Too bad to have to turn the delightful tale into a deathbed story, but the facts in the case are insistent. The decree is issued; "Thou fool, this night thy soul shall be required of thee." And thus concludes the second picture, called "Today."

But wait! What is this ghastly spectacle that startles the eye and shocks the mind with its appalling contrast? How hideous the content of the final image so hopelessly designated "Forever"! Can it be that the progeny of Yesterday is identified in this miserable wreck now cast in the final portrait? Yes, it is so! For Death, the hand-servant that Christ gave God during those dark hours on Calvary, has been about his duties. And while the grim charioteer has delivered full many who chose Christ to their heavenly home, he has found time to drive this lost soul down the frightful chasms of woe and into the kingdom of outer darkness. "And in hell he lift up his eyes, being in torments."

Time is the seedtime of eternity. It is here that we determine what we shall be out there. Two ways are before us; two choices defined; two destinies revealed. To choose the present world is to choose that which, with the vaporous years, will vanish away. For this one who "went away sorrowful" it could be no different. His greedy hands are empty and his selfish fingers hold not a cent. His gold is left behind to buy some potter's field, and earth's rich man has long since become eternity's pauper.

Death forever fixes the destiny of man. Its dagger, vibrating in the human heart, says, "He which is filthy, let him be filthy still: and he that is holy, let him be holy still." When the night of death descends on mortal flesh the day of grace is over, and the soul wings its way into the endless aeons to abide by its earth-born choice forever. And so the last chapter is closed and the pen discarded. The embers of hope turn to ashes upon the altar. The instruments of divine grace are laid away. The winged couriers of God, dispatched on many an errand of mercy, can only shave the darkness with drooping wing and sigh, "*Lost!*" He is gone! Gone to where no ray of light shall ever kindle the darkness. Gone to where no voice of cheer shall ever quiet the storm. Gone to where no kind providence shall ever mend the broken keel, or helmsman guide through the angry surges of despair and into the Haven of Rest. He would not have Christ in time; Christ will not have him in eternity! And so he is gone!

Child of destiny, this day is yours, and you must choose. Over the weary miles of the centuries He has come, and with bleeding feet and wounded hands He stands before you. The question is ever the same: "What will you do with Jesus which is called the Christ?" Will you own Him? Then shall your fainting heart own more on earth, and in the world to come, eternal life. Will you reject Him? Be ready for the inevitable. Your treasure will surely turn to trash, and your revelry to ruin. Soon you shall press the gaudy gold to your lips for one last lingering caress before it is torn from your grasp and you are plunged into the dark dungeon of despair where your only song shall be, "Soul, thou shalt never eat; thou shalt never drink; thou shalt never be merry."

The greatest mystery of all the ages will be the fact that man would not consider the infinite gain contained in Christ's promise, "Seek ye first the kingdom of God, and his righteousness; and all these things shall be added unto you."

# 33. WHY HE CAME

*This is a faithful saying, and worthy of all acceptation, that Christ Jesus came into the world to save sinners* (I Tim. 1:15).

IT IS UNIVERSALLY agreed among men of understanding that Jesus Christ is the most outstanding figure of human history. Those who discount His deity and ignore His precepts readily assent to the fact that His life made the greatest impression for good upon world society of any life ever lived. The haughty and the humble, the rich and the ragged, the favored and the forgotten mingle their varied voices in acclaim as they give to this humble Galilean first place in the scale of human achievement. Yet few are those who have bowed at the shrine of truth to discover the real purpose for which He came. Paul, first-century scholar and missionary-evangel, tarried there, and emerged from a rendezvous with Revelation to publish the most wonderful tidings of time or eternity, "Christ Jesus came into the world to save sinners."

He who preached the greatest sermons ever uttered did not come into the world primarily to preach. He who gave sight to the blind, hearing to the deaf and speech to the dumb did not come into the world primarily to heal. He whose lofty ideals and principles radiated from a sinless heart and a flawless character did not come into the world primarily to establish an example for conduct. He whose fidelity in life and courage in death will forever be incomparable did not come into the world primarily to teach men to live honestly and to die bravely. These attributes, however commendable and worthy, are insufficient to tell the motive which drove Him from realms celestial to regions terrestrial. There is one magnificent accomplishment that stands pre-eminently above all others and gives to each accompanying attainment its proper value. Spirit prompted, divinely given, faithfully recorded, it reads gloriously, "Christ Jesus came into the world to save sinners."

God's system of salvation need not be made complex. The combined facts of man's universal sinfulness and God's absolute holiness portray the need. Christ's substitutionary death provides the solution. God's holiness must of necessity manifest itself in the separation of the sinner from Himself, and coupled with the tragic truth that all men have sinned, a ransom beyond the ability of human power to afford was expedient if men were to be redeemed. How significantly, in this respect, reads the assuring Gospel, "God commendeth his love toward us, in that, while we were yet sinners, Christ died for us."

The heavenly hosts knew the real import of His visit to earth, and informed Joseph, "He shall save his people from their sins," and the shepherds, "Unto you is born this day in the city of David a Saviour, which is Christ the Lord." John the Baptist chose his introduction carefully, and to the multitudes declared, "Behold the Lamb of God, which taketh away the sin of the world." Christ's own claims give credence to such utterance, for it was He who testified of Himself, "I am come to pour out My life a ransom." We remember that it was while He spoke of the manner of this decease with the two prophets on the mountain that God's voice was heard in commendation: "This is my beloved Son: hear him!" No wonder the central message of the Early Church was that of reconciliation through the death of Christ. Those first Christians were faithful unto death in declaring the good news that on that Cross "God was in Christ, reconciling the world unto himself."

As a preacher, Christ excelled; as a teacher, He predominated; as a philosopher, He was unequaled; as a man, He was unsurpassed. Yet His prime glory lies in none of these virtues. We dare not minimize the effects of His code of ethics in elevating world-society. We dare not slight His tutelage calculated to inspire us to planes of holy principle and hallowed conduct. We dare not belittle His philosophy of love toward God and fellow man that would give us one world, a united brotherhood. We dare not ignore the perfect pattern of His life, exciting men to strive for all that is noble and best. But Christ placed the incentive for such endeavor strictly in His Cross-work and sacrificial death. It is here, and here alone, that we find that door that opens into the spiritual kingdom where all these pursuits are made possible. It is here we find that new birth and divine life without which there is no moral, spiritual or true physical victory either individually or collectively. It is here we find the only foundation that can support any and all worthy superstructure.

But still, the true meaning of His incarnation is lost if we stop here. It is in the eternal, not the temporal, realm that the real significance of His life and death is found. How futile His life and death if time absorbs all their meaning and it is not beamed into the hereafter. The Word is plain at this point, and we are not in doubt that His earthly ministry reflected in time is transcended by His atoning death which projects into eternity. Because He who was righteous became sin for us, we who are sinners can become righteous forever. Because He who was rich became poor, we through His poverty shall be made rich. Because He who ruled heaven exchanged it for earth, we shall someday exchange earth for heaven. Because He entered through a stable door and rested on a bed of straw, we shall someday be borne by the winged seraphs of God and sweep through gates of pearl to occupy our eternal mansions. He became like us, that we might become "like him; for we shall see him as he is."

That is why He came.

# 34. LET'S GET TOGETHER

*And he is the head of the body, the church* (Col. 1:18).
*Let this mind be in you . . .* (Phil. 2:5).

THE CHURCH has subjected herself to much criticism at the hands of both adversary and friend because of her evident failure to perform the task Christ gave her, that of making disciples of all nations. That great institution, designated by her Lord as the only saving factor in society, has left a sin-bound, hell-bent world, two thousand years her auditor, unsaved. Somewhere between our powerful past and pitiful present we have lost the projection of Pentecost, the challenge of early Christianity. That which was a force has become in some places a farce. Triumph has turned to tragedy. Our message is a mockery. The nations we have been sent forth to disciple remain unconvinced.

It is the charge of an increasing number of Christians that the great downfall lies in the failure of the Church to unite the forces within her. The accusation is legitimate. Five times in His Disciples' Prayer, Christ prayed that His followers might be one; but we are not one! Paul exhorted the body of believers to be of one mind and one accord; but we are of several minds and in complete discord. If we enjoy the rent veil between God and man, we certainly do not appreciate its alleviation between man and man. With heavy cords of selfishness, bigotry and pride we weave a new one, and it is a veil of iron. We reverse the sacred order, for those who once were fellow citizens of the household of Satan choose to become strangers and foreigners in the household of God. Once we warred unitedly in defense of the camp of truth; now we are at civil war among ourselves. Protagonists have given themselves to antagonism; components to opposition. Instead of cleaving, we clash! The prospects are frightening. We are divided — and a house divided against itself cannot stand.

In the Bible, God uses a metaphor to excite His Church to unity and harmony. It is simply stated: Christ "is the head of the body, the church." Whatever other implications we may derive from the type, one fact is certain: God would have all believers everywhere heed the dictates of His Son in a combined effort to carry out His command. As in the physical realm, so in the spiritual the head motivates the body. The mind speaks; the body follows. When any other state exists, there can be only one result: impotency and failure.

Picture a concert pianist endeavoring to perform with rebellious fingers. Imagine one finger saying, "I will not play the notes indicated for me, but will, rather, play only those meant for the others." Another says, "I am not satisfied with my score, so I shall not play at all." Still another says, "I do not like my fellow fingers, so I'll just go off the scale and play a little song of my own." Needless to say, the great pianist would be humiliated and his audience so chagrined over the performance that they would never return to hear him again. Yet that is the condition of the body of Christ in the world today. Heedless of the Head, each denomination, each church, each member goes about his own willful way, while a disappointed world moves on in search of that satisfaction which the Church alone can give. The great commission has become the great "omission." We have omitted essential harmony.

And yet there is danger here. We do not contend for a soft harmony built upon a cheap foundation. There are those who advocate compatibility between truth and error, and true Christians find it impossible to oblige. Harmony for harmony's sake is not the ideal. There is harmony in the graveyard — everybody's dead! There is harmony in the hospital — everybody's sick! There is harmony in the insane asylum — everybody's crazy! The harmony that would exist if the militant forces of orthodox Christianity opened their arms to the treacherous camp of modern liberalism would be even more tragic, and the Christ who said, "Be not unequally yoked together with unbelievers," does not expect such a disastrous alliance. But the differences must be abolished among those of us who are Bible-believing, blood-washed sons of God. We have one Head, one guiding Mind. We are gathered by one Spirit into one body. We have but one supreme and all-important task: to pluck brands from the burning and save souls from hell.

The solution is discovered in the Word: "Let this mind be in you, which was also in Christ Jesus." This mind, in God, planned redemption before the foundation of the world. This mind, in Christ, performed redemption two thousand years ago. This mind, in the Holy Spirit, seeks today to persuade this dying world of its need of that redemption as it appeals for right-of-way in the life of each member of the body, the Church. It is the mind that has as its one prime purpose the salvation of sinners. It is the mind that guided Christ from the courts of heaven, down the stairway of the stars and to a Bethlehem stable. It is the mind that sustained Him through the wilderness and over the rough road of human scorn to betrayal in the house of His friends. It is the mind that, given full dominance in the bloody agony of Gethsemane, put to His lips the cup which contained the aggregate sins of mankind. It is the mind that supported Him through the tortures of Pilate's judgment hall and up the cruel slopes of Golgotha to lay down His life a ransom for many. It is the mind of Almighty God abroad in the world seeking to save that which is lost. And the command is plain: "Let this mind be in you."

Certainly here, if nowhere else, is a foundation for harmony. Jesus said, "I, if I be lifted up . . . will draw all men unto me." The Cross pales our paltry purposes and becomes the beacon light on the path of the greatest service of time or eternity. Let orthodox Christians everywhere come to the Cross for their marching orders. Those orders have never changed. "Go ye into all the world, and preach the gospel to every creature . . . and, lo, I am with you alway." Herein is the total mind of Christ! And standing like a mountain peak, sovereign over all, is the Head of the Church.

# 35. THE POLESTAR OF CHRISTIANITY

*I will come again* (John 14:3).

WHEN GENERAL DOUGLAS MACARTHUR said, "I am going away, but I shall return," the American armies had lost their last foothold on Corregidor, and the future looked dark indeed for the Allies. Years later the utterance became a symbol of conquest when our armies marched down the shell-pocked streets of Manila to terminate enemy action in that theater of war. It was then that every lip, every newspaper, every radio the world around assented, "General MacArthur has returned."

But the truth, little appreciated today, is that the general but echoed the boast of a humble Galilean who lived centuries before him. It was Jesus of Nazareth who said, when taking leave of a world whose satanic forces had resisted His mission of deliverance, "I go, but I will come again." And as surely as MacArthur, with the aid of land, sea and air power, made good his declaration, so shall the Christ of God, commanding all the omnipotence of the throne of heaven, someday bring His promise to perfect fulfillment. History shall yet record the triumph of all righteous forces at His return.

Perhaps the most lucid declaration of the Lord's return was given the disciples by the Olivet angels who assured them, "This same Jesus, which is taken up from you into heaven, shall so come in like manner as ye have seen him go into heaven." If this plain statement of fact stood alone, it would be conclusive, for it is Holy Writ, and the Bible cannot lie. But the fact that the Old Testament previews Christ's second advent more often than His first, and the fact that one out of every twenty-five verses in the New Testament attests to the glorious reality of His return, leaves a dubious Bible-reading public without excuse for skepticism. God's Word is replete with repetition of this cardinal doctrine, allowing to it a space exceeded only by that given the theme of salvation through the blood of the Cross. In the Pentateuch, the Psalms and the Prophets, its presence abounds. In the Gospels, the Acts, the Epistles and the Apocalypse, God's insistence upon the imperative nature of the doctrine leaves no doubt that it is the polestar of the Christian faith.

Yet scoffers, twenty centuries removed, persist in their abortive efforts to dissuade the faithful by saying, "Where is the promise of His coming?" Let God be true and every man a liar! God has spoken and His Word is plain. Let fools dishonor the Christ who warned against the setting of dates, if they will — their counterfeiting shall never alter the value or change the validity of the fact. At a time established only in the mind of God, Jesus shall come and will tarry no longer. Bodily, visibly, suddenly will He come — in like manner as He went away. For warring nations must own the Prince of Peace; and an unruly world must receive its Ruler; and we who love Him must be made like Him and reign with Him in His kingdom of peace.

It is this fact that Christ will someday return to earth that supplies Christianity with practical vitality. Here is the basis for fulfillment of every grand promise of salvation, the weight in every warning of wrath to come; the motive behind the divine commission to disciple the earth; the incentive to purify ourselves as He is pure. It is the one excuse for the existence of the Church, and the greatest inducement to perform faithfully the task Christ placed it in the world to do. We retain or lose our power to persuade men in proportion as we regard or disregard this blessed hope. Those first Christians were not so well versed in dogma as they were in love with His appearing. Propelled by the undying hope that their Lord would yet substantiate His promise, they Christianized a pagan empire and lighted a torch that penetrated the farthest reaches of a dying world.

In these days of darkness when men grope for that which gives peace to the living and hope to the dying, may we, like those early disciples, catch the significance of His pledge, "I will come again," May it be to us a guiding ray. May it lead us, as that bright star over Bethlehem led humble hearts long ago, to the fulfillment of our fondest hopes and dreams. May it be a cleansing fire within our hearts to make us ready to greet Him. May it excite us to reap the "fields . . . white already to harvest" while it is yet day. May it comfort our hearts as we look toward that dawning when our sainted dead shall rise to meet Him in the skies. May it add to our trophies the crown of righteousness, promised to all those who love His appearing. For Jesus shall come, and every eye shall see Him, and also they that pierced Him. And in that day every knee shall bow and every tongue confess that Jesus Christ is Lord, to the glory of God.

# 36. OUR HERO—PAST AND FUTURE

*Fear not; I am the first and the last* (Rev. 1:17).

NO OTHER BOOK of the Bible is so completely shrouded in mystery as the one so paradoxically called *Revelation.* Its content tempts the suggestion that Christ's resumption of the sacred tongue of heaven caused Him to forget the mortal language of earth. Yet, in spite of the holy veil it wears, there is no more challenging Scripture to be found; nor is there a verse which more encourages faithful hearts than this text.

How timely the Patmos proclamation! John, that disciple whom Jesus loved, stood in need of heavenly disclosure. Surely the razor fangs of time had devoured every material support and left the old man desolate. We doubt not that the tight fingers of despair crushed the apostle's spirit on that occasion which found him in prayer on the Lord's Day. Be that as it may, suddenly a dazzling light broke upon his tumbled rocks, transforming them into magic halls of revelation. A voice dispelled the appalling monotony of his idle hours with thrilling pronouncement. The sun over Patmos dimmed and died in the splendor of One whose omnipotent hand lighted the torch of his heart with wondrous promise, "Fear not! I am the first and the last."

Who can sound the depths or circumscribe the boundaries to tell the message of these words? Upon the backdrop of tribulation it flared in outline celestial. It was in the apostle's heart like the warmth of an eternal fireside. It was as the breath of calm chasing upon the heels of storm. Like a thousand suns rolled into one, it burst upon the world. How it glittered and gleamed to the soul until the shadows fled away! How it glowed until the whole heart was thrilled with expectation! No longer the bitter founts of sorrow, but the sweet tears of gladness glistened on the cheek of the banished. He could not miss the meaning. Christ had been first! Christ would be last!

It was John who had recorded Christ's words, "Before Abraham was, I am . . . and whosoever liveth and believeth in me shall never die." Is it a wonder that the Christ of the vacant tomb and the Olivet ascension should seek out John to receive His confirmation? The servant had fared little better than his Lord at the hands of an unfriendly world; but the ages to come should yet declare his riches in the everlasting triumph of that Lord.

Christ was, before all, eternal. Christ will be, after all, eternal. Between the two antipodes lies the valley of sorrows: a valley God-made but man-marred. Its tragedy is written cruelly in the blood, sweat and tears that flowed from Eden's disaster. Its focal point is Calvary, the consummation of human rebellion. Let none be fooled: it is not the valley that belongs to the Lord of glory. It is the mountains that rise on either side. Time lies in the lap of the wicked one; but the eternities are Christ's.

Before a world was framed or a man fashioned from its elements, His throne was majesty and His crown was might. Nor shall the wasting years of time alter His position. When the last curtain of the years has descended and the final sun of the centuries has set, high over all His kingdom shall endure. "Thine is the kingdom" is the glorious proclamation out of which shall be fulfilled the promise, "All things are yours." Who could desire grander heritage? "I am the first!" Who could wish greater inheritance? "I am the last!"

"And he is before all things." "The light shineth in darkness; and the darkness comprehended it not." "That at the name of Jesus every knee should bow." The Christian conquest lies not in the tragic in-between but in the First and the Last. Let not the bleak crags of this present Patmos drain the vital import of His pledge, "I give unto them eternal life; and they shall never perish." Rather let the misfortunes of time accentuate the fortunes of the forevers. Let the heavenly message charge our hearts as it did that grand old warrior on the barren and friendless isle. For the morning shall dawn, for us who with patience wait for it, when holy voices shall utter, "Lift up your heads, O ye gates; and be ye lifted up, ye everlasting doors; and the King of glory shall come in." And in that day—

Jesus shall reign where'er the sun
  Doth his successive journeys run;
His kingdom stretch from shore to shore,
  Till moons shall wax and wane no more!

# 37. ALTERNATIVES

*Rejoice evermore* . . . (I Thess. 5:16).

THERE ARE THREE WORDS in the English language which summarize the reaction of every Christian to the conflicts of this life. The words are *resentment, resignation* and *rejoicing.*

Life is a battle of wills — man's in conflict with God's. God's contradictions are infinitely more powerful than man's little purposes, and since the divine mind and the human mind follow vastly different patterns, we find life to be a series of collisions. We read in the Psalms, "The steps of a good man are ordered of the Lord." Paul assures us that "all things work together for good to them that love God." It is easy to declare, "God's way is the best way": it is not always easy to consent to that way when it completely contradicts our own. Some of the circumstances that God allows to come into the lives of His children lack sweetness and make us wonder if our Heavenly Father has not forgotten to be merciful.

The Christian life is a life free from sin's penalty in so far as Christians are to be spared the horrors of an eternal hell. It certainly is not a life void of physical, emotional and mental conflicts. If we are not held responsible for Adam's sin, we surely have shared the results of his transgression. We are made to live in a world that is continually rocked by war, scarred by crime and marked with every conceivable evil. Christians become ill; Christians suffer financial reverses; Christians endure heartache and tragedy. The world, the flesh and the devil are constantly making their demands, and the trials we are called to endure sometimes reach such proportions that the strongest saints are tempted to despair.

In facing the terrific testings of this world, the Christian has three alternatives:

He can resent.

He can resign.

He can rejoice.

Whenever our lives revolve around self, God simply must break our plans. God is always constructive, and the man who resents His hand upon his life forfeits every compensating grace which, mixed with the bitter, makes the over-all picture of his life a blessed one. Strong souls are often molded through adversity, and we are to "despise not the chastening of the Lord," knowing that heavenly correction is a sign of our Father's love and care.

The majority of Christians can be placed in the second category. They simply resign themselves to their fate in morbid, fatalistic fashion, and become mopers, whiners. Depressed in spirit, they go about sad of countenance and make the world the more gloomy because of their presence in it. Swift to share their tale of woe, they find an almost sadistic delight in dampening the ardor of others and draping happy souls in the sables of their grief.

There is no true Christian victory in simply resigning one's self to the acts of Providence. The secret of victorious living is found in a human co-operation with the divine will that brings victory out of failure and joy out of deepest sorrow. It is the secret of being able to rejoice in all the situations which befall us, knowing that God does not work simply to disappoint our hopes but rather to build our souls.

No man in history had greater reason to resent the difficulties and hardships of life than the Apostle Paul. But Paul's attitude was neither that of resentment nor of resignation. His was a joyous surrender, a victorious submission to God's will. "I glory in tribulation!" he cried. He went singing and shouting on his way, finding that his greatest triumphs arose from circumstances that posed his most stringent oppositions. Despite shipwreck, imprisonment, stonings, sickness, lashings and perils of almost every mentionable nature, he lived zestfully and faced death magnificently. And by so doing he inscribed on the monument of the saints the only name that Tarsus yielded to the world — and wrote it at the top!

There are Christians who are merely Christians; and there are Christians who are champions. What's the difference? It lies in three words:

*Resent.*
*Resign.*
*Rejoice!*

# 38. WINTER

*Come before winter* (II Tim. 4:21).

JUST HOW MUCH is involved in the words "Come before winter" is to some extent a matter of speculation. The letter is addressed to Timothy, and written from the prison at Rome. Paul is anxious that his young friend remember to bring the cloak which he has left at Troas, and that he do so before the long cold sets in. Something about the dry gusts from the north, the swirling leaves of varied color seen through the passage windows, warns that autumn will soon be running out. Bleakness will settle over Rome, and the Apostle sees the need for such preparation as can be afforded. He writes for a covering for his infirm body. He writes also for books, and especially the parchments. They will help him pass the time. The entire message has a note of urgency about it. It is almost winter!

As we stand two thousand years removed from the writing, a broader picture is ours than appeared to Timothy at the letter's reception. We now understand that Paul was in the midst of his valedictory message. He was giving vent to dying words of triumph. We venture that the winter of which he wrote was not merely that season which touches earth with a wand of ice and, having put the green herb to sleep, covers its frozen bed with a blanket of soft white. In the silent hour he has heard the muffled tread and sensed the encroachment of a dim, shadowy figure upon his solitude. Terrible persecutions have come to all the Church, and their leader has been singled out for martyrdom. The cloak, the books, the parchments are not enough. Paul must have his friends. He will have company to brighten the last sad hour of earth. "Come before winter."

There is something about winter that speaks of approaching death. If man's life may be likened to the seasons of the year, it is that season which finds him covered with hoarfrost, pinched and withered, shivering at the verge of the grave. His threescore years and ten have taken him through the budding orchards of infancy's spring, the perfumed meadows of youth's summer, the ripened harvest fields of manhood's autumn. Then comes the chilled breath of age upon his reddened cheek, making it blanch. Frosty fingers pinch the forehead into furrows as gelid hands pile glacial snows upon the brow. These are those lonely years of waiting for inevitable decease, when to look ahead or back is to be reminded that earth has no enduring goal and all Time's trophies are perishable. Yesterday the green fields faded and died; tomorrow a human form will likewise wither and die, and lie at last in the same crude grave with the herb that gave it shape and visage. Amid such reflection man most needs the comfort of his remaining friends. "The time of my departure is at hand," writes Paul to Timothy. "Come before winter."

But there is something written here that makes Paul's letter glorious. The apostle sees beyond the grave.

"Henceforth there is laid up for me a crown of righteousness, which the Lord, the righteous judge, shall give me at that day," he says. The last somber hours have taken on a mysterious beauty. Beneath the snow and ice of winter lies the embryo life of spring awaiting royal birth. Soon will come the time of deliverance when warm breezes shall kiss the barren hills and fruitless boughs, and every field and forest and stream shall come to life and join in a glad anthem of resurrection. With full faith in Christ, Paul awaits such awakening in the spiritual kingdom. The grave shall not keep its prey. That which is sown in corruption must be raised in incorruption to bear no more the marks of the earthly, but the image of the heavenly. "This mortal shall . . . put on immortality." "Death is swallowed up in victory." Heaven is ahead. Reward awaits. The King and the kingdom beckon. Small wonder Paul wrote in an earlier letter, "For to me to live is Christ, and to die is gain!"

One finds himself wondering at the conversation which ensued when Timothy came to Paul, bringing the cloak, the books and the parchments. There must have been tears at the thought of parting. There may have been shouts at the hope of heavenly reunion. But one possibility seems most certain. I have fancied that the elderly man embraced his spiritual son, and, in words charged with Spirit power, admonished, "Preach the word; be instant in season, out of season." Precious to his heart was that Gospel that graced the cold winter with hope and made of death a gateway to everlasting life.

"Come before winter." It is the call of a dying world. It is a challenge to every Christian among us to share the Gospel of redeeming grace with all men of all nations, lest, coming to that "time of departure," some shall discover that the winter of life is all.

*Printed in the United States of America*